# *Vocabulary Power*

## GRADE 4



Printed in the United States of America

ISBN 0-15-320610-1

2 3 4 5 6 7 8 9 10 082 2003 2002 2001

# Table of Contents

**CHAPTER**

**CHAPTER**

**CHAPTER**

Name ______________________________

## CONNOTATION/DENOTATION

**The words in italic type in the questions below all have meanings similar to *occupation*. Each has its own connotation, or slightly different shade of meaning. Think about the way these words are used as you answer each question.**

**1.** Would you rather have an *occupation* or a *profession?* Why?

______________________________

______________________________

**2.** What title might a person have if he or she holds a high *position* in a company?

______________________________

______________________________

**3.** *Livelihood* is like *pursuit* except that ______________________________

______________________________

______________________________

**4.** Would you expect to earn more money if you had a *job* or a *specialization*? Explain why.

______________________________

______________________________

**5.** *Vocation* often has the connotation that a job matches someone's personality. What vocation would suit a person who loves numbers and mathematics?

______________________________

______________________________

Name ____________________

## SUFFIXES

**When you add *-tion* or *-ment* to a verb, you form a noun that means "the act of" or "something that." Add suffixes to each of the following words. Then write what the new word means. The first one is done for you.**

1. occupy + tion = occupation. something that keeps you occupied

2. specialize + tion = ____________. ____________

3. educate + tion = ____________. ____________

4. entertain + ment = ____________. ____________

5. employ + ment = ____________. ____________

6. define + tion = ____________. ____________

7. introduce + tion = ____________. ____________

8. invite + tion = ____________. ____________

9. inform + tion = ____________. ____________

10. enjoy + ment = ____________. ____________

Name ____________________

## ANALOGIES

**An analogy is made of two pairs of words. The words in each pair are related to each other in the same way. Choose a word that completes each analogy.**

1. *Livelihood* is to *profession* as *happy* is to ____________.
2. *Directors* are to *movies* as *editors* are to ____________.
3. *Stories* are to *writers* as ____________ are to *webmasters.*
4. *Position* is to *manager* as *vocation* is to ____________.
5. *Mail carriers* are to *letters* as *chefs* are to ____________.
6. *Pursuit* is to *farming* as *hobby* is to ____________.
7. *Musician* is to *guitarist* as *color* is to ____________.
8. *Airplane* is to *ship* as *sky* is to ____________.

## COMPARE AND CONTRAST

**To compare two items, tell how they are alike. To contrast, tell how they are different.**

1. **occupation, hobby**

   Compare: ____________

   Contrast: ____________

2. **specialization, livelihood**

   Compare: ____________

   Contrast: ____________

3. **sergeant, general**

   Compare: ____________

   Contrast: ____________

Name ___________________________________________

## SUFFIXES

▶ **When added to a noun or verb, the suffixes *-eer, -er,* and *-or* often stand for "one who." Complete the following sentences with a word from the box. Then write a definition for the word, using the example provided.**

| auctioneer | mountaineer | volunteer | jeweler |
|---|---|---|---|
| pioneer | engineer | senator | photographer |

1. The photographer used a camera with a powerful lens to take pictures of the lions. one who takes photographs
2. Long ago, trains used steam engines that were powered by coal. The train driver was called an ______________.
   ___________________________________________
3. The ______________ called for higher bids on the antique furniture.
   ___________________________________________
4. As an experienced ______________, Joel planned to climb Mt. McKinley. ___________________________________________
5. The voters re-elected the ______________ to office because of the work he had done for his state.
   ___________________________________________
6. Mrs. Green had her broken earring repaired by the ______________.
   ___________________________________________

▶ **Write the word defined below. Then write a sentence using the word.**

7. someone who offers to work without receiving payment ______________
   ___________________________________________
8. someone who settled in an area before others did ______________
   ___________________________________________

Name ____________________

## MULTIPLE-MEANING WORDS

**Read each sentence below. Then circle the letter next to the correct meaning of each underlined word.**

**1.** My neighbor is a volunteer at the hospital.
**A** a person who works without pay
**B** to give or offer readily

**2.** The scientist hopes to engineer a new type of electric motor.
**A** a person who builds machines
**B** to create and make plans for something

**3.** The United States of America pioneered space travel.
**A** to be the first to do something
**B** a person who does something before anyone else

**4.** The fire chief gives orders to the firefighters.
**A** the leader of a group
**B** most important, main

**5.** The team of mountaineers planned to hike in the Himalayas.
**A** people who climb or live on a mountain
**B** climbs mountains for enjoyment

**6.** My puppy likes to sit in my lap.
**A** the front part of the body between the waist and the knees of a seated person
**B** one time around or over the entire length of something

**7.** Brad found an injured sparrow and will nurse it back to health.
**A** a person who takes care of the sick
**B** to take care of someone or something that is ill

**8.** I am learning how to iron my own shirts.
**A** to press clothes to remove wrinkles
**B** a hard metal

Name ____________________

## DICTIONARY

▶ **For each word below, circle the letter of the pair of guide words that could be at the top of a dictionary page containing the word.**

**1.** volunteer
- **A** vision/vocabulary
- **B** vitamin/volcano
- **C** voile/votary
- **D** visitor/voice

**2.** photographer
- **F** phonics/phrase
- **G** pharmacy/photocopy
- **H** photography/piano
- **J** photon/physics

**3.** senator
- **A** school/semester
- **B** season/senate
- **C** section/separate
- **D** saddle/select

**4.** jeweler
- **F** jellyfish/jewelry
- **G** jersey/jewel
- **H** jigsaw/juggle
- **J** justice/kale

**5.** auctioneer
- **A** attack/auction
- **B** aunt/awake
- **C** audible/awful
- **D** auburn/avenue

**6.** occupation
- **F** occupy/offer
- **G** obvious/ocean
- **H** oak/occupant
- **J** occur/odd

▶ **Now, write the guide words you might find on the page that contains these words.**

**7.** equipment ____________________

**8.** chief ____________________

**9.** sandwich ____________________

**10.** livelihood ____________________

**11.** engineer ____________________

**12.** museum ____________________

Name ______________________________

## EXPLORE WORD MEANINGS

**Think about the meaning of the underlined words. Answer each question.**

1. Wilbur had barely enough time to catch the bus. At right, draw a picture of Wilbur on his way to the bus stop.

2. Although there was a chill in the air, it was virtually spring. What season was it?

______________________________

3. Jeb has two quarters, a dime, and three pennies. He wants to buy some apple juice that costs 65 cents. To have precisely the right amount of money, what does Jeb need?

______________________________

4. The strength of the bridge was measured inaccurately. Explain how you would feel about traveling across it.

______________________________

5. The park rangers reported seeing approximately 50 deer. What number could there have been?

______________________________

If they reported nearly 50 deer, how might your answer be different?

______________________________

6. Brenda has one dollar. Her notebook costs exactly 82 cents. How much change will she receive?

______________________________

7. Replace the underlined word with a synonym:
The box contains roughly 95 raisins.

______________________________

Name ______________________________

## SUFFIXES

**Write the word that is created when *-ly* is added to the adjectives below. Then write a sentence using the new word.**

**1.** approximate + ly = ______________________________

______________________________

**2.** exact + ly = ______________________________

______________________________

**3.** perfect + ly = ______________________________

______________________________

**4.** near + ly = ______________________________

______________________________

**5.** quick + ly = ______________________________

______________________________

**6.** inaccurate + ly = ______________________________

______________________________

**7.** strong + ly = ______________________________

______________________________

**8.** Make your own *-ly* word and use it in a sentence.

__________ + __________ = ______________________________

______________________________

______________________________

Name ______________________________

## GRADIENT ANALYSIS

**On the lines provided, arrange each group of words in the order asked for.**

From least accurate to most accurate: precisely, virtually, barely, roughly

______ ______ ______ ______

From smallest to largest: small, tiny, average, minute

______ ______ ______ ______

From January to November: spring, autumn, summer, winter

______ ______ ______ ______

From longest to shortest: yard, foot, mile, inch

______ ______ ______ ______

Name ________________________________________

## CLASSIFY/CATEGORIZE

**Cross out the word in each group that doesn't belong. Then name the category on the line. The first one is done for you. Add your own word to each category.**

1. farming manufacturing fishing ~~walking~~

   types of work; building

2. business commerce trade leisure

   ________________________________________

3. budget income factories expenses

   ________________________________________

4. profit debt loan credit

   ________________________________________

5. economics ecosystem economy economist

   ________________________________________

6. capital currency cash spending

   ________________________________________

7. resources materials supplies antiques

   ________________________________________

8. factories farms orchards crops

   ________________________________________

Name ___________________________________________

## CONTEXT CLUES

**Read each sentence below. Use context clues to figure out the meaning of each underlined word. Circle the letter of the correct meaning.**

1. Jim wanted to know more about his business's economy. He wanted to know how its income was managed.
   - **A** customers and suppliers
   - **B** phone number and address
   - **C** management of money
   - **D** largest size of a product

2. Natural resources such as oil and timber should be used carefully.
   - **F** forests
   - **G** merchandise
   - **H** supplies
   - **J** gasoline

3. I worked out a budget so that I can buy a new bike.
   - **A** an exercise plan
   - **B** a method of getting something finished
   - **C** a savings account
   - **D** a plan for saving and spending

4. Telephones and e-mail are methods of communicating quickly.
   - **F** transporting goods
   - **G** sharing information
   - **H** cutting the amount of time
   - **J** following directions

5. Kevin and Kyle went into business together. They opened a pizza parlor.
   - **A** a venture to earn a living
   - **B** no one else's concern
   - **C** an errand
   - **D** a difficult task

Name ____________________________________________

## COMPARE AND CONTRAST

**Complete the following statements.**

1. *Tokens* are like *currency* except that ______________________________

   ____________________________________________

2. *Borrowing* is like *debt* because ______________________________

   ____________________________________________

3. *Spending* is like a *budget* except that ______________________________

   ____________________________________________

4. A *supermarket* is like a *restaurant* because ______________________________

   ____________________________________________

5. A *bank account* is like a *piggy bank* except that ______________________________

   ____________________________________________

6. *Libraries* are like *bookstores* but ______________________________

   ____________________________________________

7. *Assembled* is like *manufactured* because ______________________________

   ____________________________________________

8. *Crops* are like *livestock* because ______________________________

   ____________________________________________

9. A *manager* is like a *principal* because ______________________________

   ____________________________________________

10. An *employee* is like a *student* but ______________________________

    ____________________________________________

Name ___________________________________________

## CONTENT-AREA WORDS

**Read the words in the box. Then answer the questions below.**

| | | | |
|---|---|---|---|
| **civilization** | **arts** | **language** | **culture** |
| **cuisine** | **society** | **folklore** | **ethnicity** |

**1.** Which four words describe people as a group?

___________________________________________

___________________________________________

**2.** Which word is a label for the following:

jazz, pantomime, cinema, sculpture? ___________________

Give another example that fits this category. ___________________

___________________________________________

**3.** Which word deals with the way people communicate? ___________________

___________________________________________

Name two or three other words that belong in this group. ___________________

___________________________________________

**4.** Legends, myths, and tall tales are examples of ___________________.

Give examples of this. ___________________

**5.** The foods people eat and the manner in which they are prepared are

related to ___________________________________________.

Name some dishes from a particular culture. ___________________

___________________________________________

Name ______________________________

## WORD FAMILIES

▶ **Word families are made up of words that share the same root or base word. Read each set of words. Write the base word that the words in each set have in common.**

1. acculturate, culturist, cultural ______________________________
2. civilization, uncivilized, civility ______________________________
3. society, socialization, antisocial ______________________________
4. befriend, friendliness, friendship ______________________________
5. folktale, folk song, folksy, folklore ______________________________
6. misuse, useful, used ______________________________
7. ethnicity, ethnical, multiethnic ______________________________
8. celebration, celebrity, celebrated ______________________________
9. servant, service, serving ______________________________
10. apart, apartment, compartment ______________________________

▶ **Now read each word below and think about its word family. Write two or three words that are related to each.**

11. joy ______________________________
12. child ______________________________
13. warm ______________________________
14. happy ______________________________
15. art ______________________________
16. order ______________________________

Name ______________________________

## RELATED WORDS

**In the web below, fill in the boxes with words related to culture. Use the categories provided.**

Language

______________________
______________________
______________________
______________________

The arts

______________________
______________________
______________________
______________________

**Culture**

Cuisine

______________________
______________________
______________________
______________________

Folklore

______________________
______________________
______________________
______________________

Name ______________________________

## CLASSIFY/CATEGORIZE

**Cross out the item which does not belong in the group. Then write a name for the category on the line provided. Add your own word that fits the category.**

| | | | |
|---|---|---|---|
| **1.** diary | journal | memoir | news story |
| **2.** biography | telephone | autobiography | photograph |
| **3.** intermission | interview | quiz | interrogation |
| **4.** textbook | novel | magazine | motion picture |
| **5.** typewriter | paper | pencil | pen |
| **6.** envelope | stamp | stationery | reply |
| **7.** reader | author | publisher | editor |
| **8.** jacket | plot | spine | pages |

Name ______________________________

## GREEK ROOTS

**Many English words have been built using roots from ancient Greek. Read the roots and their meanings in the box below.**

| **Greek root** | *auto* | *bio* | *graph* | *photo* | *tele* |
|---|---|---|---|---|---|
| **Meaning** | self | life | written | light | at a distance |

▶ **Use what you already know about the following words and the information in the box to write a definition.**

1. biography ______________________________
2. autobiography ______________________________
3. autograph ______________________________

▶ **Fill in the blanks below by inserting or completing a word. Use the Greek roots above to help you.**

4. A camera uses a special film which is exposed to the light for a very brief moment. The result is a ______________.
5. A pilot is safely in the air and allows the plane to control itself. He puts it on ______________pilot.
6. The ______________vision allows us to see images such as movies that are broadcast from a distance.
7. Morse created a machine that sent written messages over a long distance. This was called a ______________, and it used an alphabet called Morse code.
8. Write your own words using the roots listed above.

______________ ______________

______________ ______________

Name ______________________________

## COMPARE AND CONTRAST

**Read the word pairs below. Identify how they are alike and how they are different. The first one has been done for you.**

**1. Saturday, Monday**

Compare: Saturday and Monday are both days of the week.

Contrast: Only Monday is a school day.

**2. biography, autobiography**

Compare: ______________________________

Contrast: ______________________________

**3. diary, memoir**

Compare: ______________________________

Contrast: ______________________________

**4. interview, test**

Compare: ______________________________

Contrast: ______________________________

**5. journal, logbook**

Compare: ______________________________

Contrast: ______________________________

**6.** Think of a pair of words that are alike in one way, but different in another. Write the pair, then compare and contrast them.

______________________, ______________________

Compare: ______________________________

Contrast: ______________________________

Name ____________________

## MULTIPLE-MEANING WORDS

**Read each sentence and the definitions of the underlined word. Circle the letter that shows which way the word has been used.**

1. After the fire all that remained of the old house was a roofless skeleton.
   **A** the main columns and beams, without walls
   **B** all the bones of a human body

2. The scientist's years of research laid the framework for his later inventions.
   **A** the beginning of a house before walls are added
   **B** a set of ideas from which to begin working

3. My sister made a pretty dessert by pouring fruit and gelatin into a heart-shaped mold.
   **A** a pan which gives food a decorative shape
   **B** a type of fungus found on damp or decaying surfaces

4. Bark and branches are part of the structure of most trees.
   **A** what something is made of
   **B** a building

5. The teenager was of a small frame and easily slipped through the railings to save the stranded puppy.
   **A** an object used for displaying a photograph or painting
   **B** the physical make-up of the body

6. The tailor uses a form so that his jackets are well-shaped.
   **A** a model of the upper body used for fitting clothes
   **B** a document with blank spaces to be filled with information

7. The composition of dark and light colors made the painting unusual.
   **A** a written essay
   **B** the way something is put together

8. In social studies we are learning about the anatomy of the government.
   **A** the way that parts are organized
   **B** the study of the parts of the body

Name ____________________

## CONTENT-AREA WORDS

▶ **Each numbered group contains special vocabulary words for a certain topic or area of study. On the line provided, write the topic or area from the box that fits the list.**

| drama | grammar | anatomy | music | social studies |
|---|---|---|---|---|

**1.** skeleton, muscles, veins ____________________

**2.** actors, stage, costumes, plot ____________________

**3.** nations, states, capitals, communities ____________________

**4.** composition, piano, treble clef ____________________

**5.** subject, predicate, sentence ____________________

| architecture | language arts | art | sports | mathematics |
|---|---|---|---|---|

**6.** subtraction, multiplication, division, patterns ____________________

**7.** paints, brushes, easels, images ____________________

**8.** football, basketball, soccer, score ____________________

**9.** framework, structure, base, foundation ____________________

**10.** speaking, listening, writing ____________________

▶ **Choose two topic or category labels from either of the boxes above. List at least four additional words related to each of the labels you chose.**

**Label:** ____________________ **Label:** ____________________

____________________ ____________________

____________________ ____________________

____________________ ____________________

____________________ ____________________

Name ____________________

## SYNONYMS

**The words in the box are synonyms for one of the words in the web below. Write each one with its synonym. One has been done for you. Add your own synonyms to the web.**

| form | character | mold | expression |
|---|---|---|---|
| identity | look | frame | individuality |

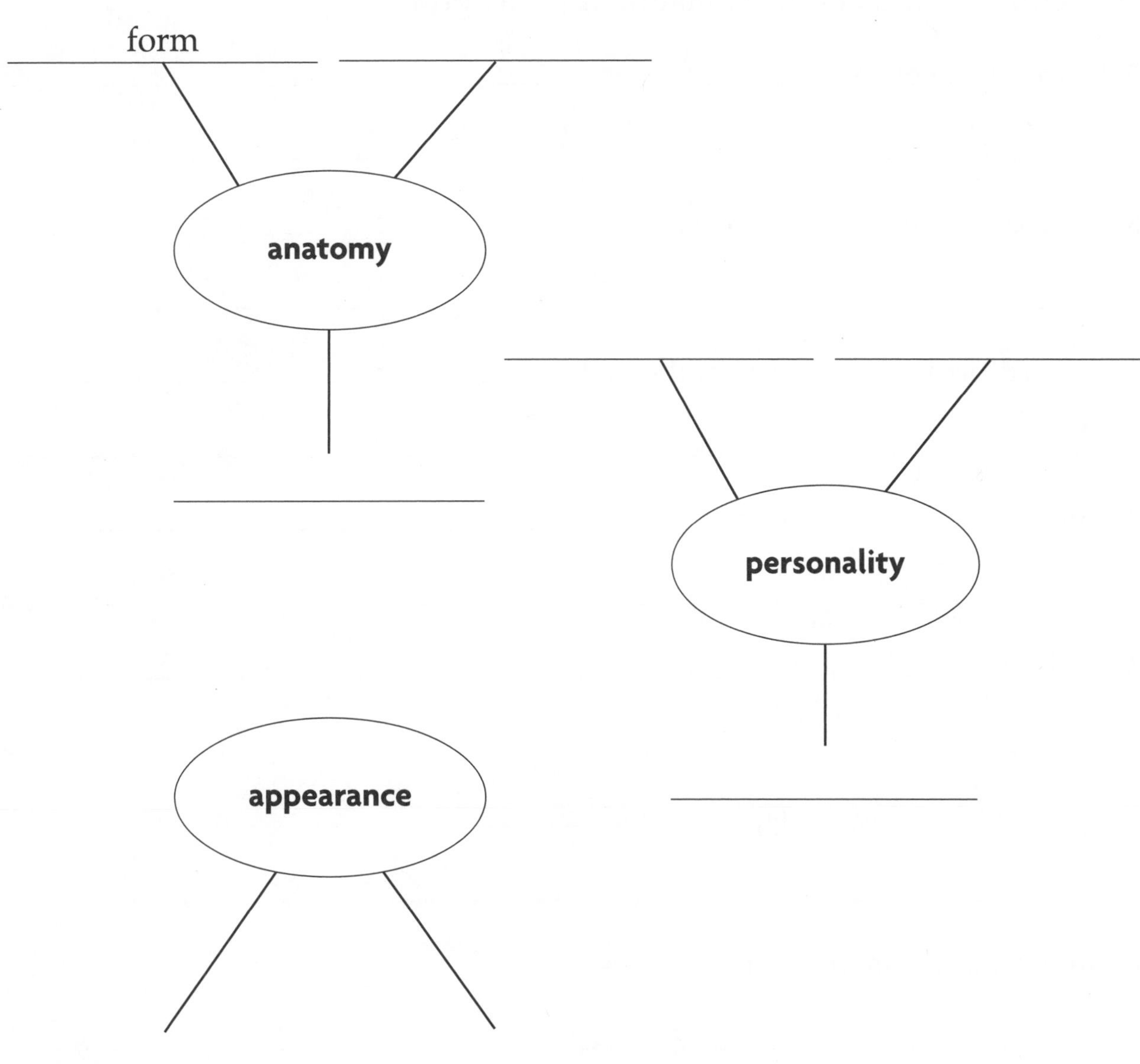

Name ______________________________

## CLASSIFY/CATEGORIZE

**Answer the following questions with a word from the box.**

| | | | |
|---|---|---|---|
| **aquatic** | **arctic** | **habitat** | **temperate** |
| **tropical** | **arid** | **alpine** | **subterranean** |

1. Which word is a label for all the others? ______________________

**Name the type of habitat in which you would find the following plants and animals. Add another inhabitant to the group.**

2. coral, fish, eels, seaweed ______________________

3. monkeys, parrots, alligators, vines ______________________

4. desert tortoises, cactuses, rattlesnakes ______________________

5. moles, earthworms, ants ______________________

6. polar bears, walruses, caribou ______________________

7. grizzly bears, deer, maple trees ______________________

8. mountain goats, pine trees, eagles ______________________

Name ______________________________

## ANALOGIES

▶ ***Analogies* are made up of two pairs of words. Each pair is related in the same way. Complete the analogies below. The first one is done for you.**

**1.** *Nest* is to *habitat* as ___oak___ is to *tree.*

**2.** *Grass* is to *cows* as ________________ are to *seals.*

**3.** *Fawn* is to ________________ as *pup* is to *wolf.*

**4.** *Burrow* is to *woodchuck* as *den* is to ________________.

**5.** *Arid* is to *desert* as ________________ is to *rain forest.*

**6.** *Jeep* is to *driving* as ________________ is to *picture-taking.*

**7.** *Arctic* is to *tropical* as *east* is to ________________.

**8.** *Yes* is to *no* as *question* is to ________________.

**9.** *Day* is to *week* as ________________ is to *year.*

**10.** *Alpine* is to ________________ as *coastal* is to *beach.*

**11.** *Mole* is to *subterranean* as ________________ is to *aquatic.*

**12.** *Huge* is to *tiny* as *whale* is to ________________.

▶ **Now try this.**

**13.** *Wolf* is to *dog* as ________________ is to ________________.

**14.** *Calf* is to *cow* as ________________ is to ________________.

**15.** *Frog* is to *amphibian* as ________________ is to ________________.

**16.** *Pasture* is to *meadows* as ________________ is to ________________.

**17.** *Camping* is to *tent* as ________________ is to ________________.

Name ____________________

## WORD FAMILIES

▶ **Read the following groups of words. Look for the root or base word in the word family. Write the root or base word.**

**1.** habitat, habitation, inhabit ____________

**2.** humanist, inhuman, human, humanitarian ____________

**3.** planetary, planet, planetarium, planetoid ____________

**4.** coloration, colorfast, colorist ____________

**5.** maximum, maxim, maximize, maximal ____________

**6.** cracker, crackle, crackleware ____________

**7.** journalism, journalist, journalize ____________

**8.** worker, workmen, overworked ____________

**9.** geology, geography, geometry, geode ____________

**10.** nonsense, sensitive, sensory, senseless ____________

▶ **Write other words that belong to the same family as each of the following. Notice that some words may fit into more than one family.**

**11.** aquatic ____________

**12.** subterranean

*sub* ____________

*terr* ____________

**13.** temperate

*temp* ____________

word part *-ate* ____________

Name ______________________________________________

## CONTEXT CLUES

▶ **The words in the box are all related to the way in which things are arranged. They are each used in slightly different ways. Choose the word that best fits each sentence below.**

| | | | |
|---|---|---|---|
| **sequence** | **arrangement** | **sequel** | **continuous** |
| **subsequent** | **organization** | **order** | **progression** |

1. A dictionary lists words in alphabetical ____________________.
2. A 24-hour television channel offers viewers a ____________________ broadcast.
3. The ushers seated the guests at the banquet according to the seating ____________________.
4. The movie was such a success that the following year the producers made a ____________________ to it.
5. Chapter 6 and the ____________________ chapters in the unit all deal with fractions.
6. We are learning about the ____________________ of events that led to the Revolutionary War.
7. The ____________________ of books at the library made it simple for patrons to find what they were looking for.
8. A steady ____________________ of spectators soon filled the stadium.



▶ **Now try this. Write a word to complete each phrase.**

9. numerical ____________________
10. ____________________ progress
11. ____________________ pages
12. ____________________ of flowers

Name ____________________

## EXPLORE WORD MEANINGS

**Think about the meaning of the underlined words. Write answers to the questions.**

1. Create a title for the sequel to "Morton Mouse Goes West."

   ____________________

2. Starting with 20, list the four subsequent multiples of 10.

   ____________________

3. Write the following in numerical order, starting with the largest.

   12, 6, 24, 10, 16 ____________________

4. List in sequence the steps you take to prepare a snack.

   **a.** ____________ **d.** ____________

   **b.** ____________ **e.** ____________

   **c.** ____________ **f.** ____________

5. What is the arrangement of desks in your classroom? Draw a rough sketch below.

Name ______________________________

## SYNONYMS

**You can make word webs of synonyms. Write each word from the box on a line around its synonym. One word is written for you.**

| | | | | | |
|---|---|---|---|---|---|
| **constant** | **following** | **advancement** | **nonstop** | **set-up** | **arrangement** |
| **pattern** | **later** | **uninterrupted** | **progress** | **headway** | **succeeding** |

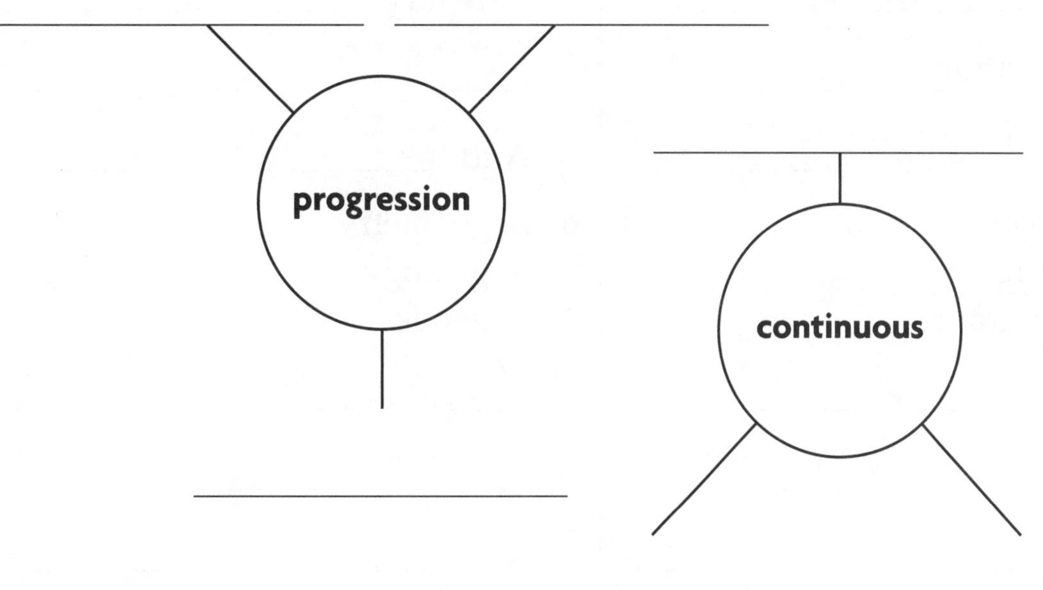


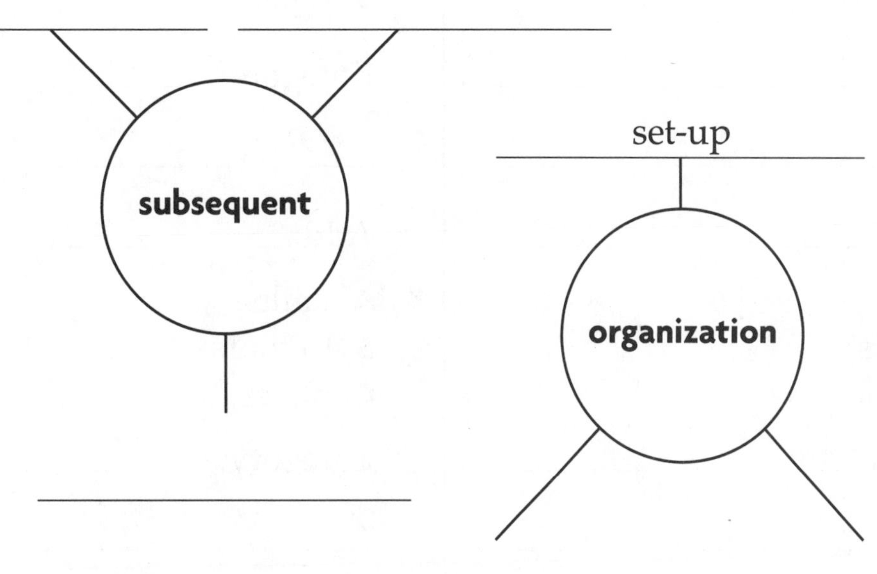

Name ____________________

## CLASSIFY/CATEGORIZE

**Read the words in each list below. Label the category to which each group belongs. Then add another word to the list. The first has been done for you.**

**1.** **A** sediment
**B** deposits
**C** rivers

Category: words related to rock formation

Add: sand

**2.** **A** magma
**B** volcanic
**C** seismograph

Category: ____________________

Add: ____________________

**3.** **A** geologist
**B** photographer
**C** geographer

Category: ____________________

Add: ____________________

**4.** **A** gravity
**B** planets
**C** rotation

Category: ____________________

Add: ____________________

**5.** **A** petroleum
**B** fossils
**C** minerals

Category: ____________________

Add: ____________________

**6.** **A** geometry
**B** geology
**C** geode

Category: ____________________

Add: ____________________

**7.** **A** granite
**B** quartz
**C** topaz

Category: ____________________

Add: ____________________

**8.** **A** faults
**B** tremors
**C** plates

Category: ____________________

Add: ____________________

Name ______________________________

## COMPARE AND CONTRAST

**Complete the following sentences to describe how the two things named are alike or different.**

1. *Summer* is like *winter* because ______________________________

2. *Petroleum* is like *gasoline* but ______________________________

3. *Gravity* is like *glue* but ______________________________

4. *Magma* is like *rock* except that ______________________________

5. A *seismograph* is like a *speedometer* because ______________________________

6. A *stalactite* is like a *stalagmite* but ______________________________

7. *The Rockies* are like *the Andes* except that ______________________________

8. A *diamond* is like a *ruby* because ______________________________

9. *Iron* is like *gold* but ______________________________

10. A *gemologist* is like a *geologist* because ______________________________

Name ______________________________

## SUFFIXES

**Complete each sentence by adding a suffix to the word in parentheses. Choose one of the suffixes from the box below. Write the new word in the sentence.**

| Suffixes | Definition |
|---|---|
| *-ed* | an action or state in the past |
| *-ic* | related to, like |
| *-ary* | connected with, relating to |
| *-ive* | doing or tending to do something |
| *-er, -ist* | a person who does something |

1. A ______________________ is a person who studies the history of the earth. **(geology)**

2. Lava is ______________________ rock. **(melt)**

3. The firefighter's actions were ______________________. **(hero)**

4. The fire ______________________ all night. **(burn)**

5. The ______________________ ash fell many miles from the eruption. **(volcano)**

6. Limestone is a ______________________ rock, formed from small pieces of other rocks. **(sediment)**

7. A strong earthquake ______________________ the seaport. **(destroy)**

8. A ______________________ studies the earth and its inhabitants. **(geography)**

Name ______________________________

## EXPLORE WORD MEANINGS

**Write the word(s) from the box that best answer the following questions.**

| **marine** | **nautical** | **maritime** | **naval** |
|---|---|---|---|
| **mariner** | **oceanic** | **coastal** | **submarine** |

**1.** Which words are related to the sea or ocean?

__________ __________ __________ __________

__________ __________ __________

**2.** Which word has to do with the land? __________

**3.** Which words are related to the Latin root *mare*, which means "sea"?

__________ __________

__________ __________

**4.** Which words come from the Latin root *navis* and the Greek root *naus*, which both mean "ship"? __________ __________

**5.** In what kind of waters could you find a submarine? __________

**6.** Which word names a sailor, or person who navigates a ship?

__________

**7.** Which words could be used in relation to the armed forces?

__________ __________ __________

**8.** Find a word that is related to *navigate*. __________

Write another word from the same family. __________

Name ____________________

## ANALOGIES

▶ **In each half of an analogy, the words in the pair are related in the same way. Think about the relationships in the following pairs of words. Then complete the analogy.**

1. *Naval* is to *navy* as ______________ is to *coast.*
2. *Fish* are to *gills* as ______________ are to *lungs.*
3. *Oceanic* is to *marine* as *damp* is to ______________.
4. A *ship* is to *nautical* as a ______________ is to *agricultural.*
5. *Lobsters* are to *maritime* as ______________ are to *arctic.*
6. A *mariner* is to a *sailor* as a ______________ is to an *instructor.*
7. *Marine* is to an *adjective* as ______________ is to a *noun.*
8. *Atlantic* is to *Maine* as ______________ is to *California.*
9. *Arctic* is to *Ocean* as ______________ is to *Sea.*
10. A *submarine* is to a *ship* as an *earthworm* is to a ______________.

▶ **Now try this. Choose two words from the box and think about their relationship to each other. Make an analogy by writing two words of your own that are related in the same way. The first one has been started for you.**

| | | | |
|---|---|---|---|
| **ship** | **sail** | **sailor** | **waves** |
| **captain** | **anchor** | **dock** | **tides** |

11. Captain is to sailor as ______________ is to ______________.
12. ______________ is to ______________ as ______________ is to ______________.
13. ______________ is to ______________ as ______________ is to ______________.

Name ____________________

## CONTENT-AREA WORDS

**A word map can show how words are related to each other. Read the following boxed words. Then look at the word map. Add words from the box to the word map by writing each word near the word it is most closely related to. One has been done for you.**

| | | | | | |
|---|---|---|---|---|---|
| fish | gulf | dunes | sharks | Atlantic | minerals |
| lobsters | oil | Pacific | bay | Indian | beach |
| Arctic | penguins | whales | oysters | seaweed | gas |

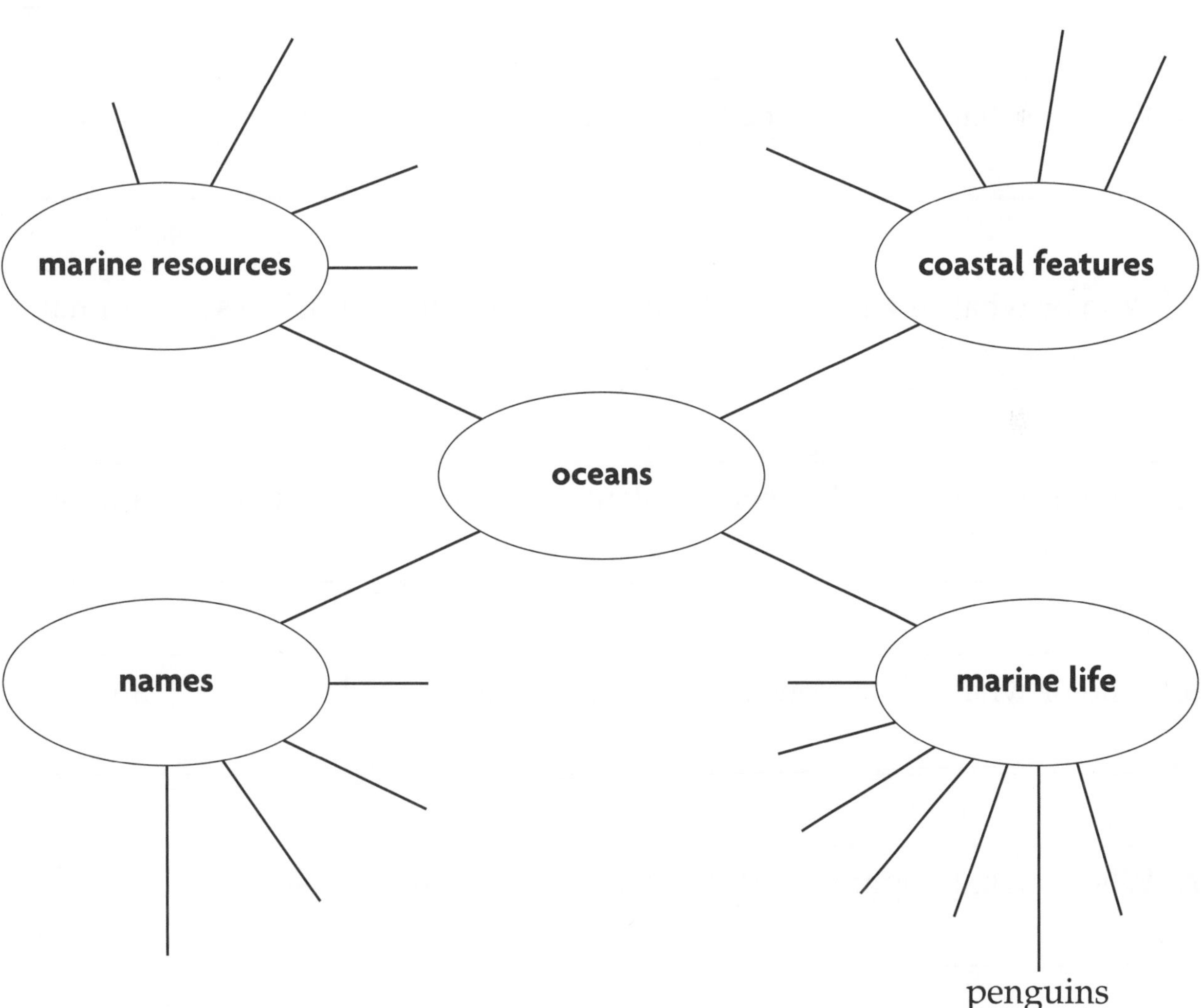

Name ______________________________

## EXPLORE WORD MEANINGS

**Answer the questions by circling all the words on the right that answer the questions. Write a sentence using the underlined word and one of the circled words.**

**1.** Who or what might <u>thrive</u>? plant person business animal

______________________________

______________________________

**2.** Who or what might <u>flourish</u>? plant person business animal

______________________________

______________________________

**3.** Who or what might <u>succeed</u>? plant person business animal

______________________________

______________________________

**4.** Who or what might <u>prosper</u>? plant person business animal

______________________________

______________________________

**5.** Who or what might <u>blossom</u>? plant person business animal

______________________________

______________________________

**6.** Who or what might <u>flower</u>? plant person business animal

______________________________

______________________________

**7.** Who or what might <u>survive</u>? plant person business animal

______________________________

______________________________

**8.** Who or what might <u>progress</u>? plant person business animal

______________________________

Name ______________________________________________

## HOMOPHONES AND HOMOGRAPHS

▶ **Homophones are words that sound the same but are spelled differently. Write the correct spelling of the word next to its definition.**

**1.** flour flower
**A** rose or tulip ____________
**B** powdery substance made from wheat ____________

**2.** hour our
**A** sixty minutes ____________
**B** belonging to us ____________

**3.** heal he'll heel
**A** he will ____________
**B** back of foot ____________
**C** make well ____________

▶ **Homographs are words that are spelled the same but are pronounced differently and have a different meaning. Write the pronunciation that matches the definition.**

**4.** pro′gress pro•gress′
**A** to move forward ____________
**B** gradual improvement ____________

**5.** re′cord re•cord′
**A** document of past events ____________
**B** to set down in writing ____________

**6.** min′ute mi•nute′
**A** sixty seconds ____________
**B** very small ____________

Name ______________________________

## CONNOTATION/DENOTATION

▶ **Rank the following groups of words.**

**1.** From least to most healthy: thrive, succeed, blossom, survive

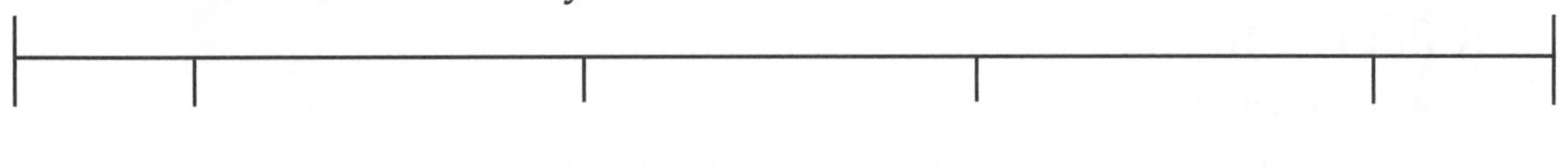

______ ______ ______ ______

**2.** From fastest to slowest: jog, sprint, run, dash

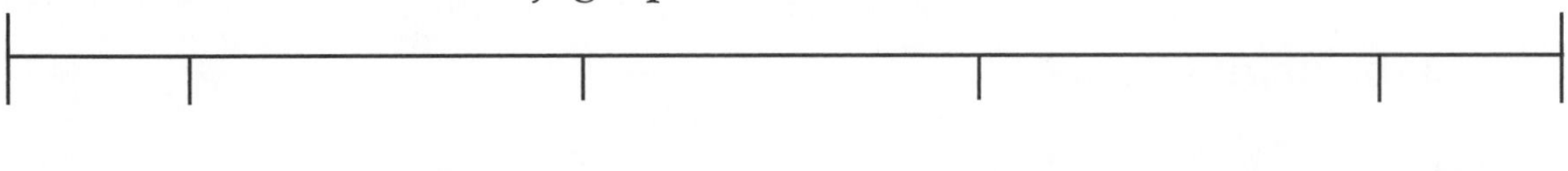

______ ______ ______ ______

**3.** From least to most noticeable: speck, blotch, spot, smudge

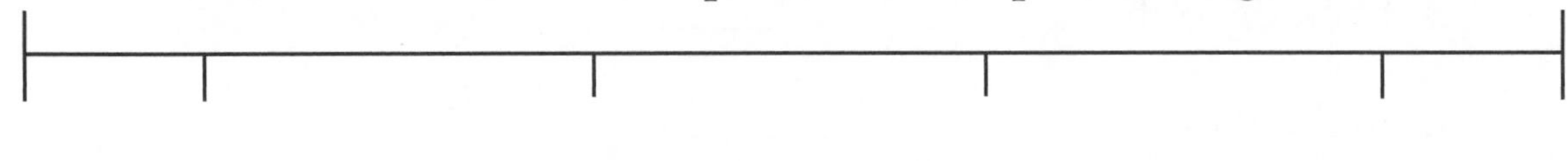

______ ______ ______ ______

▶ **The following pairs have similar meanings. Circle the word which has a more positive connotation. Explain your choice.**

**4.** flourish flower ______________________________

______________________________

**5.** prosper succeed ______________________________

______________________________

**6.** scheme plan ______________________________

______________________________

**7.** spied watched ______________________________

______________________________

Name ________________________________________________

## CONTENT-AREA WORDS

**Read the words in the box. Write each word where it belongs in the Venn diagram. Some words may fit in more than one category. Add words of your own to each category.**

| subject | easel | landscape | acrylic |
|---|---|---|---|
| canvas | bristle | impression | palette |

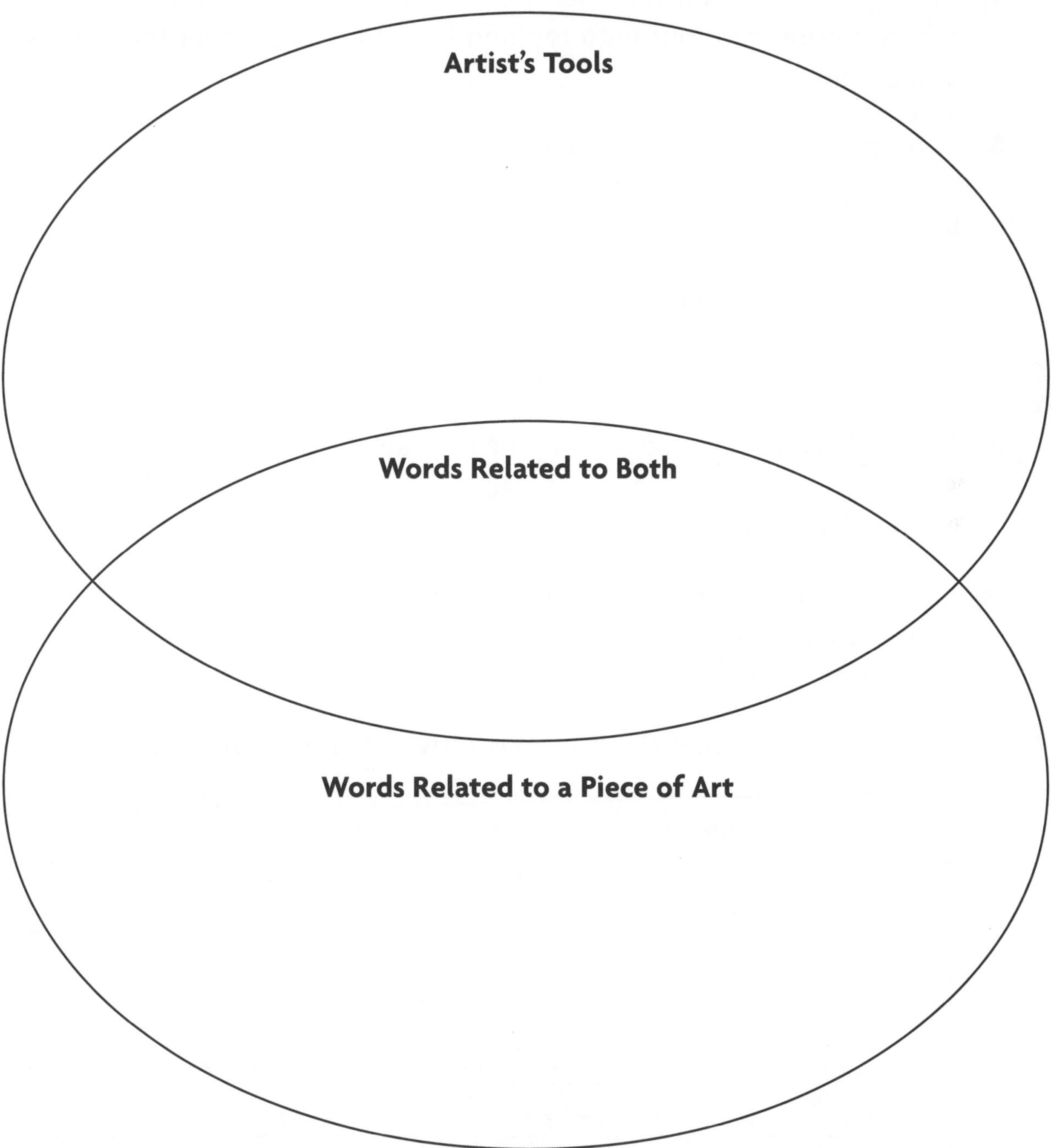

Name ______________________________

## MULTIPLE-MEANING WORDS

▶ **Read each sentence. Circle the letter for the definition that matches the underlined word.**

1. The museum bought a canvas by Vincent van Gogh.
   **A** a painting, often done with oil paints
   **B** a heavy, coarse material

2. I purchased a beautiful landscape for my living-room wall.
   **A** a computer printout with top and bottom being longer than sides
   **B** a picture of natural scenery

3. Porcupines bristle to keep enemies away.
   **A** make quills stand on end
   **B** usually animal hair used in paintbrushes

4. Robert is allergic to wool, so he wears acrylic sweaters.
   **A** a type of water-based paint
   **B** a man-made yarn

5. Helen chose fruit as the subject for her sketches.
   **A** an area of study
   **B** an object represented in art

6. Please chop the onions and the tomatoes.
   **A** to cut with a knife
   **B** a cut of meat

▶ **Choose two words from the box. Write two meanings for each.**

| steer | model | post | yarn | mold |
|---|---|---|---|---|

7. ______________________________

______________________________

8. ______________________________

______________________________

Name ______________________________

## ANALOGIES

▶ **Each pair of words in an analogy is related in the same way. Complete the following analogies.**

1. An *easel* is to an *artist* as a *camera* is to a ______________.
2. An *impression* is to ______________ as an *image* is to *seeing.*
3. *Paint* is to *palette* as *film* is to ______________.
4. A *meadow* is to a *landscape* as a ______________ is to a *portrait.*
5. *Canvas* is to *fabric* as ______________ is to *vehicle.*
6. *Bristle* is to *whistle* as ______________ is to *wink.*
7. *Pale* is to *vibrant* as ______________ is to *wild.*
8. *Texture* is to *bumpy* as *sound* is to ______________.
9. A *sculptor* is to a *sculpture* as a ______________ is to a *cake.*
10. *Artistic* is to *art* as ______________ is to *music.*
11. *Show* is to *hide* as *tall* is to ______________.
12. *Knead* is to ______________ as *carve* is to *wood.*

▶ **Now try this. Create the second half of the analogy by choosing two words that are related in the same way as the first pair of words.**

13. A *zebra* is to a *horse* as a(n) ______________ is to a(n) ______________.
14. *Canada* is to *North America* as ______________ is to ______________.
15. *Colorful* is to *drab* as ______________ is to ______________.
16. ______________ is to ______________ as *hurry* is to *worry.*

Name ____________________

## EXPLORE WORD MEANINGS

▶ **Read the words in the box. Then use them to answer the questions.**

| | | | |
|---|---|---|---|
| **fable** | **fiction** | **literature** | **poetry** |
| **myth** | **nonfiction** | **narrative** | **folktale** |

**1.** Which one word is a label for all the others? ____________________

**Now write the word that is a label for the following features.**

**2.** has animals who behave like humans; teaches a lesson

____________________

**3.** true stories or facts about real life; purpose may be to inform

____________________

**4.** a story that was first told orally; is passed down and often retold in slightly different ways ____________________

**5.** did not really happen, but may seem realistic; may be fantasy; usually for entertainment ____________________

**6.** may have rhythm and rhyme; uses figurative language to create images ____________________

**7.** uses story structure; may be about an actual event

____________________

**8.** fictional story from long ago; tries to explain why things are the way they are ____________________

▶ **Now try this. Write the title of a piece of literature and choose the word from the box above that labels it.**

Title ____________________

Genre or Label ____________________

Name ______________________________

## ANALOGIES

An analogy is made up of two pairs of words. Each pair of words is related in the same way. For example: *"Hot* is to *cold* as *tall* is to *short."*

▶ **Look at each pair of words below. Decide how the words are related. Then complete the analogy.**

1. *Literature* is to ______________ as *dance* is to *ballet.*
2. *Award* is to *prize* as *little* is to ______________.
3. *Folktale* is to *storyteller* as *song* is to ______________.
4. *Author* is to *writer* as *eat* is to ______________.
5. *Poetry* is to *poet* as ______________ is to *playwright.*
6. *Diary* is to *journal* as *candy* is to ______________.
7. *Fable* is to *instructional* as ______________ is to *entertaining.*
8. *Narrative* is to *story* as *giggle* is to ______________.
9. *Famous* is to *unknown* as *rough* is to ______________.
10. *Myth* is to *fantasy* as ______________ is to *reality.*

▶ **Now try this. Think about the relationship between the two words provided. Then add another pair of words to complete the analogy.**

11. *Keyboard* is to *pencil* as ______________ is to ______________.
12. *Leave* is to *stay* as ______________ is to ______________.
13. *Spring* is to *season* as ______________ is to ______________.
14. ______________ is to ______________ as *kitten* is to *cat.*

Name ___________________________________________

## ANTONYMS

An antonym of a word can be formed by adding a prefix.

| ***un-* and *non-* mean "not"** |
|---|

▶ **Add a prefix to each of the words below to form its antonym.**

**1.** _______ + fiction = ______________________________

**2.** _______ + realistic = ______________________________

**3.** _______ + natural = ______________________________

**4.** _______ + flammable = ______________________________

▶ **For each of the following word pairs, draw pictures to illustrate the differences between the antonyms. For example, draw the covers and create titles for a fiction and a nonfiction book.**

| **5.** fiction nonfiction | **6.** noisy quiet |
|---|---|
| **7.** addition subtraction | **8.** alone together |

Name ___________________________________________

## SYNONYMS

▶ **Match the words in the box with their synonyms.**

| | | |
|---|---|---|
| **opportunity** | **serendipity** | **circumstance** |
| **occurrence** | **chance** | **probability** |

1. likelihood ______________________
2. chance ______________________
3. incident ______________________
4. good fortune ______________________
5. situation ______________________
6. luck ______________________

▶ **Replace the underlined words with a synonym from the box.**

| | | |
|---|---|---|
| **chance** | **happenstance** | **airplane** |
| **occasion** | **probability** | **auditorium** |

7. It was chance that led me to a career in music.

   ______________________

8. Mark took advantage of the opportunity to travel to Alaska.

   ______________________

9. The town's one-hundredth anniversary was an important event.

   ______________________

10. There was a lot of excitement as the hall filled with guests.

   ______________________

11. The mayor had been out of town. He returned home in a jet.

   ______________________

12. The likelihood of rain was very slight, so the opening ceremony was held outdoors. ______________________

Name ______________________________

## CLASSIFY/CATEGORIZE

**In each group below, one word does not belong to the same category as the others. Circle the letter of that word. Then classify the remaining words by writing a label for that group.**

**1.** **A** serendipity
**B** happenstance
**C** fortune
**D** calamity

______________________________

______________________________

**2.** **F** occasion
**G** occurrence
**H** mystery
**J** event

______________________________

______________________________

**3.** **A** opportunity
**B** occasion
**C** chance
**D** advertisement

______________________________

______________________________

**4.** **F** forecast
**G** stormy
**H** overcast
**J** cloudless

______________________________

______________________________

**5.** **A** snow
**B** icicles
**C** sleet
**D** hurricane

______________________________

______________________________

**6.** **F** hill
**G** patio
**H** mountain
**J** slope

______________________________

______________________________

**7.** **A** sergeant
**B** corporal
**C** sailor
**D** captain

______________________________

______________________________

**8.** **F** ice cream
**G** milk
**H** cheese
**J** bread

______________________________

______________________________

Name ______________________________

## WORDS IN CONTEXT

| **chance** | **circumstance** | **probability** |
|---|---|---|
| **opportunity** | **occurrence** | |

**Fill in the blanks to complete the weather forecast. Use each word only once.**

1. Today there is a 90 percent ______________________ of rain, so take your raincoats and umbrellas!
2. Don't expect it to clear up before the weekend. The ______________________ of its continuing to rain is high.
3. Under these ______________________s, flooding is likely in low-lying areas.
4. This is a strange ______________________ for this time of year, which, as you know, is usually dry.
5. By next week, the rains should stop, and your gardens will have an ______________________ to dry out a bit.

## DICTIONARY

**Read the paragraph. Use the underlined words to add labels to the example of a dictionary page. Use the information in the paragraph to figure out where to place each label.**

The two words at the top of a dictionary page are called guide words. These are the first and last words on the page. Each entry word is listed in dark type. Following each entry word is a phonetic respelling of the word. This shows how to pronounce or say the word. Next is the part of speech. This is often abbreviated. Finally, the definition of the word is given.

opportunity — orange

**op•por•tu•ni•ty** [op•ər•t(y)o͞o′nə•tē] *n.* A right or convenient time, occasion, or circumstance

Name ___________________________________________

## CLASSIFY/CATEGORIZE

**In each group below, three words are related and one is not. Determine what category the words belong to, and then circle the letter of the word that does not belong. Add another word that fits the category.**

**1.** **A** choreographer
**B** conductor
**C** program
**D** usher

Category: ______________________

Add: ______________________

**2.** **F** compose
**G** orchestrate
**H** perform
**J** performance

Category: ______________________

Add: ______________________

**3.** **A** entertain
**B** audience
**C** please
**D** delight

Category: ______________________

Add: ______________________

**4.** **F** choreograph
**G** chorus
**H** telegraph
**J** graphite

Category: ______________________

Add: ______________________

**5.** **A** conduct
**B** orchestra
**C** tutu
**D** cello

Category: ______________________

Add: ______________________

**6.** **F** scarf
**G** boots
**H** mittens
**J** sandals

Category: ______________________

Add: ______________________

**7.** **A** cycling
**B** tennis
**C** baseball
**D** football

Category: ______________________

Add: ______________________

**8.** **F** peach
**G** potato
**H** strawberry
**J** pineapple

Category: ______________________

Add: ______________________

Name ______________________________

## SUFFIXES

**The suffixes *-er, -or,* and *-ist* added to a verb change the meaning to "one who." Read below and follow the directions.**

"City Performing Arts" is planning a grand performance for the opening of its downtown theatre.

▶ **Give a title to the person or people who will do the following:**

1. choreograph the dance number ______________________
2. conduct the orchestra ______________________
3. compose original music for the opening act

   ______________________
4. perform in the dance or drama acts ______________________

▶ **Think of other people who might be needed. Write the verb that tells what he or she does and add a suffix. Remember that the audience does not see all the people involved in making the performance a success.**

**For example: drum + er = drummer**

5. ____________ + ____________ = ______________
6. ____________ + ____________ = ______________
7. ____________ + ____________ = ______________
8. ____________ + ____________ = ______________

▶ 9. What is the word meaning "one who entertains"? ______________

10. Can an *entertainer* be a *volunteer*? Why or why not? ______________

    ______________________________

11. Can an *entertainer* be a *pioneer*? Why or why not? ______________

    ______________________________

Name ______________________________

## COMPARE AND CONTRAST

▶ **Think about the meanings of the underlined words in each question. Answer with complete sentences.**

1. Would you prefer to entertain or to be entertained? Why?

______________________________

______________________________

2. Which task is more complicated: to orchestrate or to conduct? Explain.

______________________________

______________________________

3. At a musical recital, would you prefer to be in the audience or be a performer? Explain. ______________________________

______________________________

▶ **In each of the following pairs, compare and contrast the meanings of the words by noting how they are similar and how they are different. The first has been done for you.**

4. **performer, choreographer**

   Compare: related to dancing or movement on stage

   Contrast: The choreographer does not perform in front of the audience.

5. **composer, violinist**

   Compare: ______________________________

   Contrast: ______________________________

6. **guitar, drum**

   Compare: ______________________________

   Contrast: ______________________________

Name ______________________________

## RELATED WORDS

**The words in the box are all related to *carousel*. Look at the web below and decide which category each word fits. Write the words where they belong. Add some words of your own.**

| | | | |
|---|---|---|---|
| **gilded** | **carnival** | **rotating** | **ornate** |
| **musical** | **whirligig** | **melodious** | |

**Where You See It**

______________________________

______________________________

______________________________

**What You Hear**

______________________________

______________________________

______________________________

**carousel**
synonym(s):

______________________________

______________________________

**Movements It Makes**

______________________________

______________________________

______________________________

**What You See**

______________________________

______________________________

______________________________

Name ______________________________

## CONTEXT CLUES

**Use context clues to complete the following sentences. Write a word from the box. Then explain how you chose that answer.**

| carousel | whirligig | melodious | gilded | rotating |
|---|---|---|---|---|

1. The spinning top had a whirling motion. Grandpop says that in his day they called it a ______________.

   Explain: ______________________________

   ______________________________

2. Jim watched for his bright-red backpack on the baggage ______________ as an orange one circled past again and again.

   Explain: ______________________________

   ______________________________

3. The carousel horse had streaks of gold in its mane and tail. Its saddle and bridle were also ______________ and shone brightly in the sun.

   Explain: ______________________________

   ______________________________

4. The harpist played a lovely melody, and the singer's ______________ voice matched it perfectly.

   Explain: ______________________________

   ______________________________

5. As the Earth orbits the Sun, it is also ______________ on its axis. It is this turning action that gives us night and day.

   Explain: ______________________________

   ______________________________

Name ___

## COMPARE AND CONTRAST

▶ **Fill in the chart below. In the first column, put an X in each box that correctly describes a carousel horse. In the second column, put an X in each box that describes a real horse.**

| | carousel horse | real horse |
|---|---|---|
| four legs | | |
| life size | | |
| smaller than life size | | |
| stays in one place | | |
| moves around freely | | |
| natural colors | | |
| painted colors | | |
| mane | | |
| tail | | |

**Use the information from the chart to complete the lists below.**

| Similarities | Differences: Carousel Horse | Differences: Real Horse |
|---|---|---|
| **1.** ___ | **4.** ___ | **7.** ___ |
| **2.** ___ | **5.** ___ | **8.** ___ |
| **3.** ___ | **6.** ___ | **9.** ___ |

▶ **Complete the following comparisons/contrasts.**

**10.** *Musical* is like *noisy* except that ___

___.

**11.** *Carnival* is like *celebration* because ___

___.

**12.** *Ornate* is like *pretty* except that ___

___.

Name ______________________________

## RELATED WORDS

▶ **Write words from the box to label the parts of the drawing below.**

| pedestal | plaque | monument | dedication |
|---|---|---|---|

▶ **Use the words in the box to complete the sentences. Then follow the directions in 2 and 3.**

| podiatrist | scaffold | sculpt | pedestrian |
|---|---|---|---|

1. An artist hired to ______________ a statue is called a sculptor.
2. The statue needs to be restored. On the left side, draw a ______________ for the maintenance crew to climb onto.
3. The statue is in the town square. Draw a ______________ walking by.
4. One of the work crew hurt his foot and has to go to a ______________, or a foot specialist.

Name ____________________________________________

## GREEK AND LATIN ROOTS

**Look at the Latin roots in the box below and their meanings. Knowing these common roots can sometimes help you figure out the meaning of an unfamiliar word.**

| Latin root<br>Meaning | *cent*<br>hundred | *tri*<br>three | *quad*<br>four | *-ian*<br>one who |
|---|---|---|---|---|
| Greek root<br>Meaning | *-iatry*<br>art of healing | *ped* or *pod*<br>foot | *meter*<br>measure | |

▶ **Complete the *ped/pod* web below. Read the definitions and use the roots provided above to write the word described.**

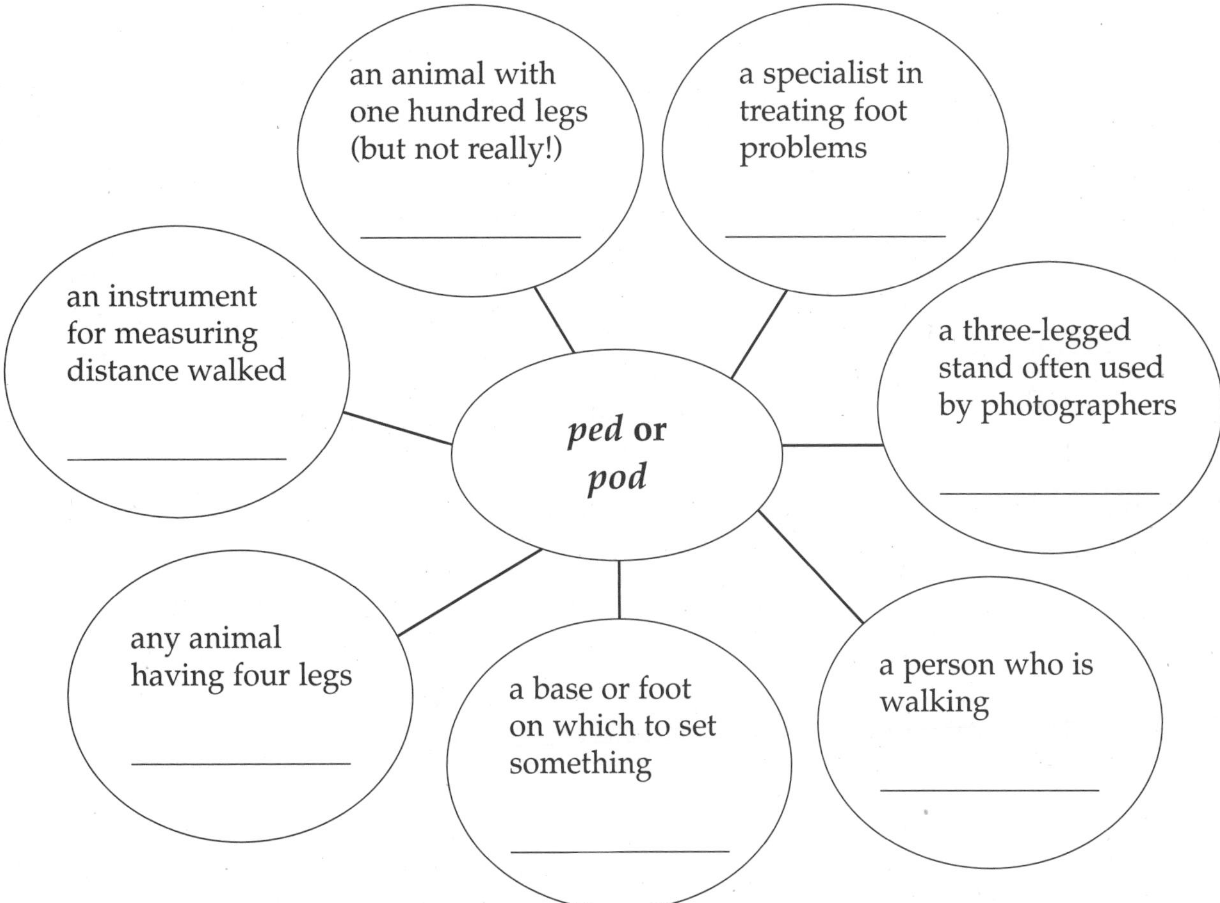




▶ **Now list other words of your own that use any of the roots above.**

________________________________________________________________

________________________________________________________________

Name ____________________

## EXPLORE WORD MEANINGS

**Think about the meaning of the underlined words. Then write your answer to each question.**

1. Other than on a statue, where might you see a dedication? ____________________

2. What purpose does a monument have? ____________________

   Who or what would you build a monument for? Explain your reasons.

3. Name materials an artist might use to sculpt a figure. ____________________

4. A scaffold is a platform raised above ground or floor level. Why would a scaffold be useful in building a monument? ____________________

5. Other than a dedication, what might be written on a plaque? ____________________

6. What would a monumental earthquake be like? ____________________

Name ______________________________

## EXPLORE WORD MEANINGS

▶ **Write each of the words from the box under the categories below. Some words may fit in more than one category.**

| vapor | surroundings | climate | smog |
|---|---|---|---|
| ozone | atmosphere | ambiance | oxygen |

**Science words**

______________________________
______________________________
______________________________
______________________________
______________________________

**Weather words**

______________________________
______________________________
______________________________
______________________________
______________________________

**Describes the area around you**

______________________________
______________________________
______________________________
______________________________

**Words with two syllables**

______________________________
______________________________
______________________________
______________________________

▶ **Now answer these questions. Think about the meaning of the underlined words.**

1. Would you prefer to breathe oxygen or smog? Explain why.

______________________________

2. How is a restaurant's ambiance similar to its surroundings? How is it different? ______________________________

______________________________

Name ______________________________

## MULTIPLE-MEANING WORDS

**Determine the meaning of the underlined word as it is used in each sentence. Write the letter of the definition that matches each.**

1. The smoke from vast forest fires added to the pollution of the atmosphere. _____
   There was an atmosphere of sportsmanship when the opposing teams met for the first time. _____
   **A** the layer of air surrounding the earth
   **B** the surrounding feeling of an environment

2. Citrus trees, such as the orange and tangerine, grow best in a tropical climate. _____
   The townspeople couldn't get enough of Yulee's Yummy Yogurt. The climate was right for Yulee to open a second store. _____
   **A** an atmosphere or feeling among people
   **B** a region having particular weather conditions

3. Ron felt homesick at first, but he soon felt comfortable in his new surroundings. _____
   The trees surrounding the lake were tall and leafy, providing shade for campers. _____
   **A** enclosing on all sides
   **B** the conditions around you

4. Jerome auditioned for the lead part in the musical. _____
   Songbirds and crickets are among the musical animals that live in the woods. _____
   **A** a dramatic performance that includes singing
   **B** melodious, sounding like music

Name ____________________

## CLASSIFY/CATEGORIZE

**In each of the following groups, three of the words are related in some way. Circle the letter of the one word that is not part of the group. Then name the category and add another word that fits.**

**1.** **A** stream
**B** waterfall
**C** glacier
**D** brook

Category: ____________________

Add: ____________________

**2.** **A** oxygen
**B** hydroplane
**C** hydrogen
**D** ozone

Category: ____________________

Add: ____________________

**3.** **A** vapor
**B** sand
**C** fumes
**D** gases

Category: ____________________

Add: ____________________

**4.** **A** ambiance
**B** mood
**C** joyfulness
**D** atmosphere

Category: ____________________

Add: ____________________

**5.** **A** cozy
**B** circle
**C** uncomfortable
**D** crowded

Category: ____________________

Add: ____________________

**6.** **A** atmosphere
**B** spherical
**C** sphinx
**D** biosphere

Category: ____________________

Add: ____________________

**7.** **A** fog
**B** haze
**C** cloud
**D** warmth

Category: ____________________

Add: ____________________

**8.** **A** jumping jacks
**B** on foot
**C** bus
**D** bicycle

Category: ____________________

Add: ____________________

Name ____________________

## GREEK AND LATIN ROOTS

**Many English words are borrowed from other languages. In Greek, the root *astro* means "star" or "star-shaped." Think about this information as you write answers for the following questions.**

1. *Nautical* comes from the Greek word for *sailor*. What does *astronaut* mean?

   ____________________

2. The endings *-ics*, *-ogy*, and *-y* mean "the science or practice of." What does *astronautics* mean?

   ____________________

   What is *astronomy*?

   ____________________

3. The suffix *-er* often means "a person who." What does an *astronomer* do?

   ____________________

4. If a *cuboid* is an object shaped something like a cube, what do you think an *asteroid* is?

   ____________________

5. If *nautical* means "having to do with the sea," what do you think *astral* means?

   ____________________

6. A dome is a rounded roof. What might an *astrodome* be used for?

   ____________________

   ____________________

7. An aster is a type of flower. Draw what you think it might look like.

8. An asterisk is a kind of punctuation mark. Draw what you think it might look like.

Name ____________________

## COMPARE AND CONTRAST

**Complete the following statements.**

1. An *astronomer* is like a *geographer* except that ____________________

____________________

2. An *asterisk* is like a *question mark* because ____________________

____________________

3. An *aster* is like a *zinnia* because ____________________

____________________

4. *Binoculars* are like a *telescope* except that ____________________

____________________

5. *Mars* is like *Jupiter* except that ____________________

____________________

6. *Dusk* is like *dawn* because ____________________

____________________

7. *Sunshine* is like *moonlight* but ____________________

____________________

8. A *space shuttle* is like an *airplane* except that ____________________

____________________

9. *Stars* are like a *galaxy* except that ____________________

____________________

Name ______________________________

## RELATED WORDS

**Words can be related in several ways. They may have the same suffix or prefix, the same root word, or similar meanings. Circle the letter of the word that is NOT related to the others in each list. Then identify the category or relationship of the other words.**

1. **A** astronaut
   **B** astrodome
   **C** astray
   **D** astronomer

   ______________________________

2. **F** astronomy
   **G** geology
   **H** story
   **J** chemistry

   ______________________________

3. **A** nautical
   **B** naughty
   **C** astronautics
   **D** aeronautics

   ______________________________

4. **F** astronomical
   **G** gigantic
   **H** enormous
   **J** size

   ______________________________

5. **A** energy
   **B** energize
   **C** energetic
   **D** enemy

   ______________________________

6. **F** rotation
   **G** rotten
   **H** rotating
   **J** rotary

   ______________________________

7. **A** aster
   **B** asterisk
   **C** astern
   **D** asteroid

   ______________________________

8. **F** vertical
   **G** horizontal
   **H** diagonal
   **J** astral

   ______________________________

9. **A** gas
   **B** gases
   **C** gash
   **D** gaseous

   ______________________________

10. **F** sunrise
    **G** sunup
    **H** dusk
    **J** dawn

    ______________________________

Name ____________________

## RELATED WORDS

▶ **Write each word from the box where it belongs.**

| | | | |
|---|---|---|---|
| **auditory** | **nocturnal** | **perception** | **extra-sensitive** |
| **ocular** | **olfactory** | **diurnal** | **extraordinary** |

Labels for senses

____________________

____________________

____________________

Labels for time

____________________

____________________

Means "out of the ordinary"

____________________

Means "unusually sensitive"

____________________

Synonym for *sense*

____________________

▶ **Choose a word from the box above to complete each sentence.**

**1.** *Audible* means "can be heard." The ____________ sense is related to the ears.

**2.** *Oculist* is a synonym for *optometrist*. The ____________ sense is related to the eyes.

**3.** *Olfaction* is the sense of smell. The ____________ sense is related to the nose.

Name ______________________________

## PREFIXES

▶ **The prefix *extra-* comes from a Latin root that means "beyond" or "outside of." Use this information to complete the following.**

1. extra = beyond or outside of    curricular = related to the curriculum

   extra + curricular = ______________________________

   What is an extracurricular activity? ______________________________

   ______________________________

   List some examples. ______________________________

2. extra = beyond or outside of    mural = having to do with walls

   extra + mural = ______________________________

   What are extramural sports competitions? ______________________________

   ______________________________

3. Complete the equation to form a word that means "beyond the ordinary."

   __________ + __________ = __________

4. Mike's dad likes to cook chili, but his chili is hotter than the usual. He cooks with unusually hot peppers. His chili is outside of the ordinary. It is *extraordinarily* hot! That's not an easy word to say, so he just calls it extra-hot. Draw a picture of someone tasting extra-hot chili.

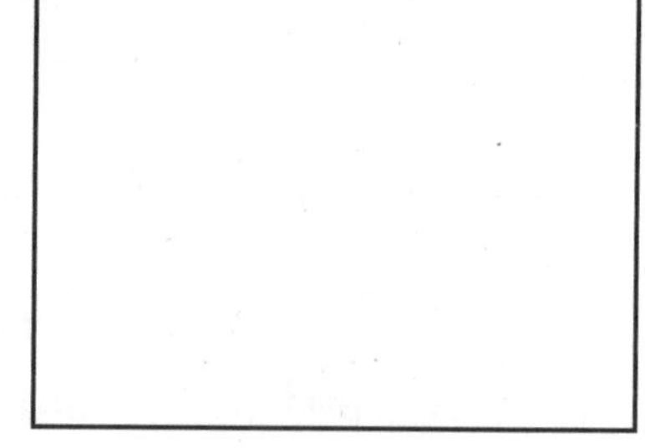

▶ ***Extra* is a shortened form of *extraordinary*. With a hyphen, it can be used as a prefix to mean "unusually." In the sentences below, write your ideas.**

5. Dogs have a good sense of smell. Extra-sensitive noses are good for

   ______________________________

6. Extra-sensitive hearing means that bats are able to ______________________________

   ______________________________

Name ______________________________

## ANALOGIES

▶ **The words in each half of an analogy are related in the same way. Determine the relationship between one pair of words. Then complete the analogy.**

**1.** *Auditory* is to the *ear* as *ocular* is to the ________________.

**2.** *Olfactory* is to *perfume* as ________________ is to *wind chimes.*

**3.** An *owl* is to *nocturnal* as ________________ is to *diurnal.*

**4.** *Perception* is to *perceive* as *reception* is to ________________.

**5.** *Extraordinary* is to *commonplace* as *sprinting* is to ________________.

**6.** A *bat* is to *wings* as a *fish* is to ________________.

**7.** A *mane* is to a *horse* as *whiskers* are to ________________.

**8.** A *nose* is to *sniff* as *eyes* are to ________________.

**9.** *Fingers* are to *toes* as a *wrist* is to an ________________.

**10.** An *eagle* is to *vision* as ________________ is to *swiftness.*

**11.** *Glove* is to *hand* as ________________ is to *foot.*

**12.** *Sharp* is to *dull* as *bright* is to ________________.

▶ **Now try this. The first half of the analogy is provided. Write a pair of words that is related in the same way.**

**13.** An *alligator* is to a *reptile* as ________________ is to ________________.

**14.** *Seeing* is to *hearing* as ________________ is to ________________.

**15.** *Water* is to a *pond* as ________________ is to ________________.

**16.** *Bear* is to *cub* as ________________ is to ________________.

Name ___

## CONTEXT CLUES

**Read each sentence, paying attention to the underlined word. On the line, write the word's meaning.**

1. We went to the arboretum to see the rare trees and shrubs.

   *Arboretum* means ___.

2. In botany class, we studied about plants.

   *Botany* means ___.

3. The botanist carefully studies the leaves and roots of the plant.

   *Botanist* means ___.

4. Oaks, pines, and many smaller plants make up the flora of our area.

   *Flora* means ___.

5. The warm greenhouse had a variety of delicate tropical plants.

   *Greenhouse* means ___.

6. The farmer grew flowers and vegetables in her garden.

   *Garden* means ___.

7. The cows grazed in the lush valley, as there was little vegetation on the barren hillsides.
   *Vegetation* means ___.

8. The botanical setting had many flowers and trees.

   *Botanical* means ___.

9. When the rosebushes bloom, they will produce beautiful red flowers.

   *Bloom* means ___.

Name ______________________________

## CLASSIFY/CATEGORIZE

**Things that are alike in some way can be classified. The name of the category tells how the things are alike. Write each of the words from the box below under the correct heading. Then add three words of your own to each category.**

| | | |
|---|---|---|
| **foliage** | **flourish** | **arboretum** |
| **nature preserve** | **botanical garden** | **greenhouse** |
| **flora** | **prosper** | **roots** |
| **thrive** | **vegetation** | **blossom** |

| Things a Botanist Studies | Places a Botanist Might Work | Words to Describe the Way Healthy Plants Grow |
|---|---|---|
| ____________ | ____________ | ____________ |
| ____________ | ____________ | ____________ |
| ____________ | ____________ | ____________ |
| ____________ | ____________ | ____________ |
| ____________ | ____________ | ____________ |
| ____________ | ____________ | ____________ |
| ____________ | ____________ | ____________ |

Name ______________________________

## COMPARE AND CONTRAST

**Complete the following statements.**

1. *Botany* is like *biology* except that ______________________________
______________________________.

2. A *garden* is like a *greenhouse* because ______________________________
______________________________.

3. A *botanist* is like a *geologist* except that ______________________________
______________________________.

4. An *arboretum* is like a *forest* except that ______________________________
______________________________.

5. A *flower stem* is like a *tree trunk* because ______________________________
______________________________.

6. *Flora* is like *vegetation* because ______________________________
______________________________.

7. An *evergreen* is like a *deciduous tree* except that ______________________________
______________________________.

8. An *aster* is like a *rose* because ______________________________
______________________________.

9. An *oak tree* is like a *pine tree* except that ______________________________
______________________________.

10. A *garden* is like a *farm* because ______________________________
______________________________.

Name ________________________________________

## CONTENT-AREA WORDS

**Read the words in the box. Determine which category each word belongs in. Write the words in the web below. Then add your own words to each category.**

| | | | |
|---|---|---|---|
| **barren** | **abrasion** | **wear** | **gravel** |
| **windswept** | **glacier** | **weathering** | **coastline** |

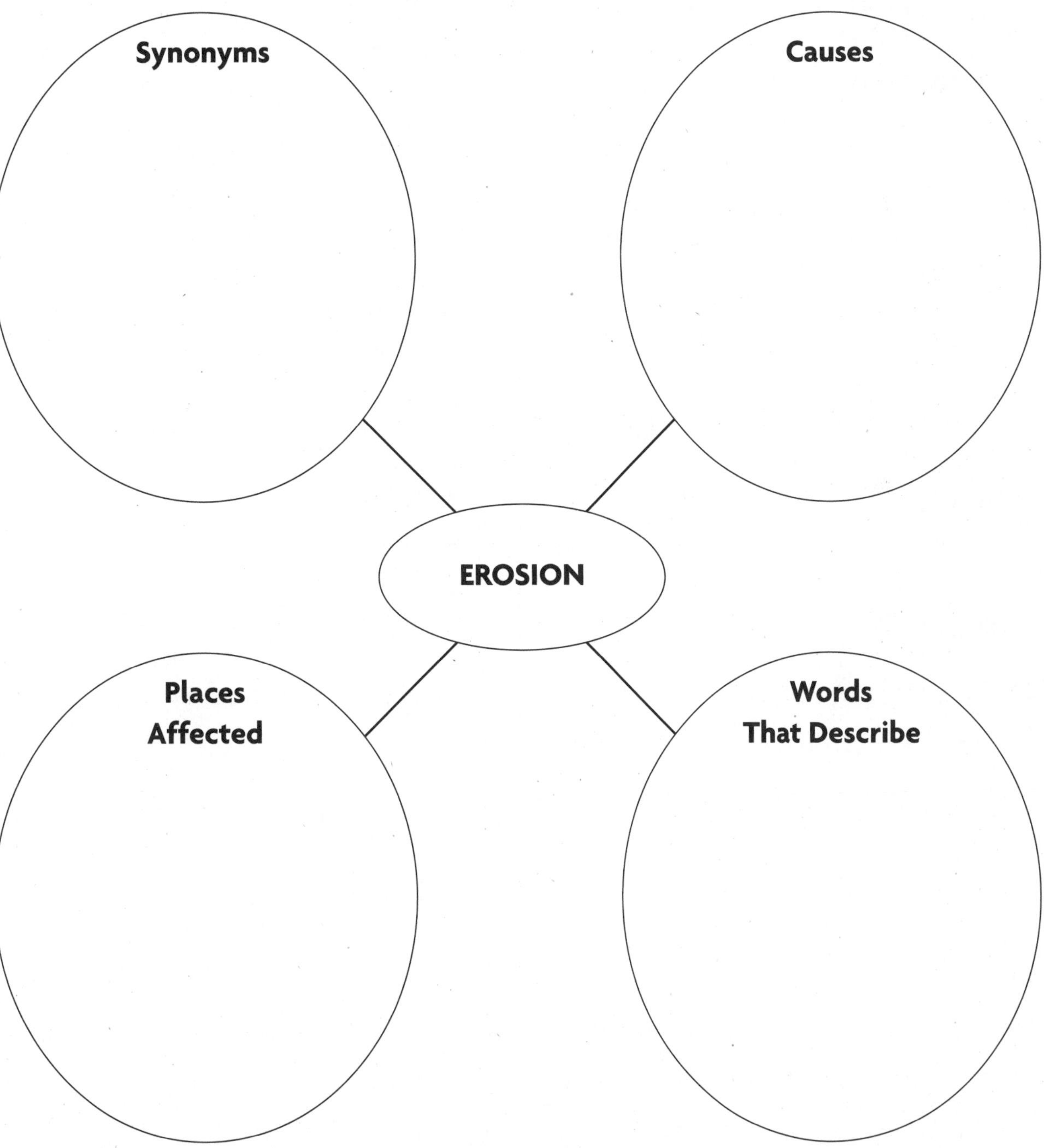

Name ______________________________

## ANALOGIES

**An analogy makes a comparison. Think about the relationship between the words in the first pair. Circle the letter of the word that best completes each analogy.**

**1.** *Wear* is to *erosion* as *cyclone* is to _____.
- **A** drizzle
- **B** blizzard
- **C** sunshine
- **D** tornado

**2.** *Sand* is to *dunes* as _____ are to *mountains.*
- **F** streams
- **G** clouds
- **H** rocks
- **J** trees

**3.** *Abrasion* is to *gravel* as *irrigation* is to _____.
- **A** water
- **B** soil
- **C** sand
- **D** clouds

**4.** *Furnace* is to *cold* as _____ is to *hot.*
- **F** slippers
- **G** glacier
- **H** bulb
- **J** sun

**5.** *Rain* is to *snow* as _____ is to *ice.*
- **A** cold
- **B** hard
- **C** water
- **D** clear

**6.** *Desert* is to *sandy* as *arctic* is to _____.
- **F** icy
- **G** far
- **H** sweltering
- **J** rainy

**7.** *Grains* are to _____ as *droplets* are to *rain.*
- **A** boulders
- **B** shells
- **C** grass
- **D** sand

**8.** *Blew* is to the *wind* as _____ is to a *volcano.*
- **F** fell
- **G** erupted
- **H** clapped
- **J** struck

Name ____________________

## SYNONYMS AND ANTONYMS

▶ **Words with nearly the same meaning are called *synonyms*. Replace each underlined word with a synonym from the word box. Write the new sentences.**

| **weathering** | **coastline** | **inquired** | **simple** |
|---|---|---|---|

1. We asked about the cause of the landslide.

   ____________________

2. Huge waves pounded the shore.

   ____________________

3. Science is an easy subject for me.

   ____________________

4. The old cabin showed signs of wear.

   ____________________

▶ **Words that have opposite meanings are called *antonyms*. Replace each underlined word with an *antonym* from the word box to change the meaning of the sentence. Write the new sentences.**

| **erosion** | **windswept** | **difficult** | **refused** |
|---|---|---|---|

5. Harsh winds had resulted in conservation of the soil.

   ____________________

6. We climbed a steep and sheltered cliff.

   ____________________

7. I struggled to answer the easy question.

   ____________________

8. My mom agreed to give me dessert before dinner.

   ____________________

Name ______________________________

## SYNONYMS

▶ ***Devastate* was used in each sentence below, but it is not the best word. Choose the synonym from the box that best fits the meaning of the sentence.**

| harm | spoil | destroy | obliterate |
|---|---|---|---|

1. The dog will not devastate you.

______________________________

2. A tornado can devastate houses.

______________________________

3. A raging fire can completely devastate a forest, leaving only ashes.

______________________________

4. Too much salt will devastate the taste of the soup.

______________________________

▶ **Replace *rebuild* with a better synonym from the box.**

| refurbish | renovate | restore | revive |
|---|---|---|---|

5. We will rebuild the old house, making it look new.

______________________________

6. We will clean the painting to rebuild it to its original beauty.

______________________________

7. A mug of hot chocolate will rebuild the cold, tired children.

______________________________

8. We will add some new curtains and a coat of paint to rebuild the room.

______________________________

Name ______________________________

## WORD FAMILIES

**Word families are made up of words that have the same root or base word. Read the words below. Circle the letter of the word that does not belong. Then replace it with a word of your own.**

**1.** **A** demolish
**B** demolition
**C** demolishing
**D** detract

______________________

**2.** **F** dessert
**G** destroy
**H** destroyer
**J** destroys

______________________

**3.** **A** devastate
**B** vest
**C** devastation
**D** devastated

______________________

**4.** **F** obliterate
**G** obliteration
**H** object
**J** obliterating

______________________

**5.** **A** refurbish
**B** refurbishes
**C** furniture
**D** refurbished

______________________

**6.** **F** renovate
**G** renown
**H** renovation
**J** renovated

______________________

**7.** **A** resistance
**B** restoration
**C** restore
**D** restored

______________________

**8.** **F** revive
**G** revived
**H** revives
**J** revisit

______________________

Name ______________________________

## EXPLORE WORD MEANINGS

**Read and respond to each question or statement.**

1. How would you **revive** a plant that is drooping? ______________________________

______________________________

Draw pictures of the plant before and after it was revived.

Before | After

2. What things might you do to **refurbish** your bedroom? ______________________________

______________________________

Draw pictures of your bedroom before and after it is refurbished.

Before | After

3. If a storm were to devastate a community, what are some things that would need to be done to **restore** it? ______________________________

______________________________

Draw pictures of the community before and after it was restored.

Before | After

Name ____________________

## COMPARE AND CONTRAST

▶ **Describe urban and rural communities by checking each box that applies. Remember that rural areas also have small towns.**

| | boulevard | lane | skyscraper | ranch | downtown | city center | subway | civic | municipal | metropolitan | agriculture | commerce |
|---|---|---|---|---|---|---|---|---|---|---|---|---|
| Urban | | | | | | | | | | | | |
| Rural | | | | | | | | | | | | |

▶ **Make a list showing how an urban community is like a rural community. Make two lists showing their differences. Use the information from the chart.**

### Likenesses

____________________

____________________

____________________

____________________

### Differences

**Urban**

____________________

____________________

____________________

____________________

____________________

**Rural**

____________________

____________________

____________________

____________________

____________________

Name ______________________________

## COMPOUND WORDS

Compound words are made up of two words. The two words may be joined together, hyphenated, or kept separate.

**For example:** armchair old-fashioned ice cream

▶ **Form two more compound words using part of the first word given.**

1. armchair — arm ________ arm ________
2. downtown — ________ town ________ town
   down ________ down ________
3. skyscraper — sky ________ sky ________
4. watercolor — water ________ water ________

## COINED WORDS

Before the first skyscraper was built, the word *skyscraper* did not exist. The word was coined, or invented, because a name was needed for this new type of building. As new ideas or inventions appear, people need to create new words. For example, most of the words related to computers are new words.

▶ **Read the descriptions below and write the word from the box that matches each.**

| **webmaster** | **pixel** | **byte** | **Internet** |
|---|---|---|---|

1. a unit of data ________
2. the person in charge of creating and maintaining a website ________
3. one spot out of thousands on a computer screen, out of which pictures are formed ________
4. an international collection of computer networks ________

Name ______________________________

## CONNOTATION/DENOTATION

▶ **Rank the following groups of words in the correct order.**

**1.** From shortest to tallest: house, skyscraper, tent, apartment building

______ ______ ______ ______

**2.** From smallest to greatest: civic, municipal, federal, state

______ ______ ______ ______

**3.** From most passengers to fewest passengers: bicycle, subway, car, bus

______ ______ ______ ______

**4.** From narrowest to widest: boulevard, highway, footpath, avenue

______ ______ ______ ______

▶ **Think about the meaning of the underlined words. Then answer each question, giving reasons for your answer.**

**5.** Would you prefer to live in an <u>urban</u> area or a <u>metropolitan</u> area?

Why? ______________________________

______________________________

**6.** Would you prefer to own a <u>skyscraper</u> or a <u>highrise</u>? Why?

______________________________

**7.** Would you prefer to walk along a <u>road</u> or a <u>boulevard</u>? Why?

______________________________

Name ______________________________

## EXPLORE WORD MEANINGS

▶ **Write the word(s) from the box that best answer the questions that follow.**

| heritage | legacy | inheritance | ancestor |
|---|---|---|---|
| history | heredity | genealogy | origin |

1. What word names a relative who lived long ago?

   ____________________

2. Which three words are related to the Latin root *heres*, which means "heir"? ____________________ ____________________

   ____________________

3. Which word means "the study of one's family history"?

   ____________________

4. This word means "the place where something began."

   ____________________

5. Which word means "the study of the past"? ____________________
6. Which words mean "something handed down from previous generations"? ____________________ ____________________
7. Which word means the opposite of *descendant*?

   ____________________

▶ **Synonyms sometimes have slightly different denotations. Write the word that best fits the definition below.**

**genealogy** **history**

**A** includes stories about what people were like and what they did

____________________

**B** a record of names, dates, and places of birth, marriage, and death

____________________

Name ______________________________

## CONTEXT CLUES

**Read each sentence and think about the meaning of the underlined word. Write a definition for the word as it is used in the sentence.**

1. The origin of Trina's family name was uncertain, but it seemed to be Scandinavian.

   *Origin* means ______________________________

   ______________________________.

2. Bradley is proud of his Scottish heritage, and is learning to play the bagpipes.

   *Heritage* means ______________________________

   ______________________________.

3. One of Shawna's ancestors fought in the American Civil War.

   *Ancestors* means ______________________________

   ______________________________.

4. My grandmother is researching her genealogy. She wants to find the first American in the family.

   *Genealogy* means ______________________________

   ______________________________.

5. Black hair and green eyes are part of my heredity from my father's side of the family.

   *Heredity* means ______________________________

   ______________________________.

6. This antique nightstand is my mother's inheritance from her grandmother.

   *Inheritance* means ______________________________

   ______________________________.

Name ______________________________

## CLASSIFY/CATEGORIZE

▶ **In each list of words below, three words belong to the same category and one does not. Circle the letter of the word that does not belong. Name the category for the other words, and then add another word that fits.**

**1.** **A** legacy
**B** heritage
**C** inheritance
**D** descendants

Category: ______________________

Add: ______________________

**2.** **F** skating
**G** mathematics
**H** science
**J** history

Category: ______________________

Add: ______________________

**3.** **A** genealogy
**B** cardiology
**C** geography
**D** biology

Category: ______________________

Add: ______________________

**4.** **F** language
**G** physical traits
**H** customs
**J** fruit trees

Category: ______________________

Add: ______________________

**5.** **A** photographs
**B** trains
**C** birth certificates
**D** letters

Category: ______________________

Add: ______________________

**6.** **F** Native American
**G** Egyptian
**H** Canada
**J** Korean

Category: ______________________

Add: ______________________

▶ **Now try this. Create your own categories, and list three items that fit.**

**7.** **A** ______________________

**B** ______________________

**C** ______________________

Category: ______________________

**8.** **A** ______________________

**B** ______________________

**C** ______________________

Category: ______________________

Name ______________________________

## CONTEXT CLUES

**Read the following story. Use context clues to help you choose the correct word from the box. Fill in the blanks, using each word only once.**

| | | | |
|---|---|---|---|
| **transatlantic** | **transcontinental** | **translate** | **transparent** |
| **transmountain** | **transoceanic** | **transport** | **translucent** |

Josh and Henry decided to travel around the world and visit many countries. They started their world tour in West Africa. They traveled by ship across the Atlantic Ocean. The ______________________ journey took two weeks. The cabin they stayed in had a ______________________ window, so although it let sunlight into the room, they could not see the outside.

They docked in New York City, and soon after began their travels across the North American continent. Eventually, they reached San Francisco, on the west coast. Their ______________________ journey was long but a lot of fun.

They had especially enjoyed their ______________________ hike across the Rocky Mountains. Once, they stopped at a mountain spring with crystal-clear water. They had never seen such a ______________________ pool. Josh had wanted to ______________________ some of the water back home, but they still had far to go.

From California, the men needed to cross the ocean once again, to get to Japan. This time they decided to fly. The ______________________ journey was much faster by plane than by ship! In Japan, they needed someone to ______________________ for them in the restaurant. They were very glad to find a waiter who spoke English!

Name ____________________

## EXPLORE WORD MEANINGS

**Read and answer each question. Think about the meaning of the underlined word.**

1. You are going on a <u>transatlantic</u> journey. What type of transportation would you prefer and why?

   ____________________

   ____________________

   Where would your journey begin and where would it end?

   ____________________

2. You are going on a <u>transcontinental</u> journey. What continent will you travel through? Name some sights you hope to see there.

   ____________________

   ____________________

3. What does <u>transpacific</u> mean?

   ____________________

4. What would be a good way to <u>transport</u> a case of lightbulbs?

   ____________________

   ____________________

5. How might one make a <u>transmountain</u> trip?

   ____________________

   ____________________

6. Would you prefer the windows in your home to be <u>transparent</u> or <u>translucent</u>? Explain your reasons.

   ____________________

   ____________________

Name ______________________________

## WORD FAMILIES

**Words that share the same root, base word, prefix, or suffix belong to a word family. Read the word families below. Write the root, base word, prefix, or suffix for each family.**

1. transcontinental, continentalism, continental ______________
2. economist, economics, economically ______________
3. settlement, resettlement, settler ______________
4. transoceanic, oceanography, oceanfront ______________
5. informational, informatively, informant ______________
6. marina, mariner, aquamarine ______________
7. explainable, explanation, explanatory ______________
8. glaciology, glacial, glaciation ______________
9. analyst, analytics, analysis ______________
10. geologist, geological, geologize ______________
11. mountainous, transmountain, mountaineer ______________
12. strategize, strategist, strategic ______________
13. transparent, translate, translucent ______________
14. sequential, sequentially, sequencing ______________
15. relative, relationship, relatedness ______________
16. transport, deportation, import ______________
17. urbane, urbanite, suburban ______________
18. disinterested, interestingly, uninteresting ______________

Name ____________________

## RELATED WORDS

**Use the words from the box to answer the questions that follow.**

| | | | |
|---|---|---|---|
| **irrigate** | **trough** | **canal** | **moisten** |
| **aqueduct** | **hydrate** | **sluice** | **drench** |

**1.** Four words that are synonyms for "to water."

________________ ________________

________________ ________________

**2.** Which would you do regularly, as on a farm? ________________

**3.** Which would you do if the soil were just slightly dry? ________________

________________

**4.** Which would you need to do if the soil were extremely dry?

________________

**5.** Four words that are ways to hold or carry water.

________________ ________________

________________ ________________

**6.** Which one has a gate to control the flow of the water? ________________

**7.** Which one can be small enough to bring water to fields, or large enough for ships to sail on? ________________

**8.** Write your own words related to water.

________________ ________________ ________________

________________ ________________ ________________

________________ ________________ ________________

Name ______________________________

## WORD FAMILIES

▶ **Words related by a root or base word belong to the same family. Circle the letter of the word that is not related to the others in the list.**

1. **A** irrigate
   **B** irrigation
   **C** irrigating
   **D** irritate

2. **F** moisten
   **G** moisturize
   **H** moist
   **J** mostly

3. **A** hybrid
   **B** hydrate
   **C** dehydrated
   **D** hydrant

4. **F** aqueduct
   **G** aquifer
   **H** acquire
   **J** aquarium

▶ **Words can also be related by structural elements such as prefixes, suffixes, or word parts. Circle the letter of the word that is not related to the others in the list. Then add your own to the list.**

5. **A** runner
   **B** jumping
   **C** throwing
   **D** playing

   Add: ______________________

6. **F** independent
   **G** incorrect
   **H** island
   **J** indirect

   Add: ______________________

7. **A** regularly
   **B** rapidly
   **C** energy
   **D** frequently

   Add: ______________________

8. **F** redo
   **G** reach
   **H** rerun
   **J** reheat

   Add: ______________________

9. **A** ouch
   **B** out-yell
   **C** outwalk
   **D** outswim

   Add: ______________________

10. **F** fields
    **G** tigers
    **H** mittens
    **J** mint

    Add: ______________________

Name ____________________________________________

## CONTEXT CLUES

**Context clues can help you determine the meaning of an unfamiliar word. Read the following sentences. Write a definition for the underlined word. Look for clues in the other words in the sentence.**

1. In dry parts of the country, farmers use irrigation to bring water to their crops. ____________________________________________

2. A canal was built, leading from the lake to the farthest field, to bring water to the crops.

   ____________________________________________

3. Farmers must be very knowledgeable about the climate, or weather conditions, in their area.

   ____________________________________________

4. We needed a heavy rain to drench the vegetable garden before it dried out completely.

   ____________________________________________

5. When the apples are ripe, farmers harvest them and take them to market.

   ____________________________________________

6. If you want to raise crops and farm animals, you should study agriculture in college.

   ____________________________________________

7. As the stream had dried up, we kept a trough filled with water for the cows to drink.

   ____________________________________________

8. When there is enough water in the canal, the sluice is closed.

   ____________________________________________

Name ______________________________

## RELATED WORDS

**Around the web are definitions of words related to rivers. Fill in each blank with a word from the box that matches the definition.**

| delta | inlet | meander | valley |
|---|---|---|---|
| oasis | tidal | tributary | source |

**river**

______________ a low point between hills or mountains

______________ a stream that feeds into a larger stream or river

______________ the beginning point

______________ to follow a winding course

______________ a fertile area in a desert, often along a riverbank

______________ the flat area of land at the mouth of a river

______________ a narrow strip of water leading into land from the ocean

______________ having to do with the ocean tides

Name ____________________

## COMPARE AND CONTRAST

**Complete the following sentences to describe how the two items in italics are alike or how they are different. The first has been done for you.**

**1.** A *delta* is like a *plain* because they are both flat and they both support crops.

**2.** A *river* is like a *stream* except that ____________________.

**3.** *To meander* is like *to flow* but ____________________.

**4.** A *tributary* is like a *branch* because ____________________.

**5.** A *water fountain* is like an *oasis* because ____________________.

**6.** A *canyon* is like a *valley* but ____________________.

**7.** An *inlet* is like a *harbor* except that ____________________.

**8.** A *snow flurry* is like a *drizzle* because ____________________.

**9.** A *tidal pool* is like a *pond* except that ____________________.

Name ______________________________

## ANALOGIES

▶ **An analogy is made of two pairs of words. The words in each pair are related in the same way. Complete the following analogies.**

1. *Tidal* is to the *tides* as *seasonal* is to ____________.
2. *Source* is to *origin* as *instrument* is to ____________.
3. The *Nile* is to *Africa* as the ____________ is to *North America.*
4. A *delta* is to the *end* as ____________ is to the *beginning.*
5. A *river* is to *natural* as ____________ is to *man-made.*
6. *Saltwater* is to ____________ as *freshwater* is to *lakes.*
7. ____________ is to *liquid* as *glacier* is to *solid.*
8. *Dry* is to *rain forest* as ____________ is to *desert.*

▶ **Now try this. For each analogy, choose at least one word from the box. Complete a pair of related words. Then write another pair that is related in the same way.**

| forest | ocean | coastline | windswept |
|---|---|---|---|
| climate | foliage | landscape | wind |

9. ____________ is to ____________

as ____________ is to ____________.

10. ____________ is to ____________

as ____________ is to ____________.

11. ____________ is to ____________

as ____________ is to ____________.

Name ____________________

## CLASSIFY/CATEGORIZE

**In each group below, the words or phrases are all related to a word from the box. Write the word that labels the category. Add an animal or a descriptive phrase that fits each category.**

| | | | |
|---|---|---|---|
| **amphibian** | **arachnid** | **vertebrate** | **mammal** |
| **crustacean** | **reptilian** | **amphibious** | **invertebrate** |

**1.** **A** tiger
**B** ape
**C** wolf

Category: ____________________

Add: ____________________

**2.** **A** crow
**B** fox
**C** trout

Category: ____________________

Add: ____________________

**3.** **A** scorpion
**B** daddy longlegs
**C** tick

Category: ____________________

Add: ____________________

**4.** **A** tortoise
**B** lizard
**C** snake

Category: ____________________

Add: ____________________

**5.** **A** toad
**B** salamander
**C** newt

Category: ____________________

Add: ____________________

**6.** **A** usually aquatic
**B** outer shell
**C** may have claws

Category: ____________________

Add: ____________________

**7.** **A** jellyfish
**B** earthworm
**C** octopus

Category: ____________________

Add: ____________________

**8.** Write an adjective that describes something that lives or works both on land and in the water

____________________

Name ______________________________

## WORD FAMILIES

**Words may be related by a root or base word, or by word parts. For each group below, determine what word part the words have in common. Then add another word that belongs to the same family. The first has been done for you.**

**1.** **A** amphibious
**B** amphitheatre
**C** amphipod

Family: *amphi-*

Add: amphibian

**2.** **A** amphibian
**B** veteran
**C** German

Family: ______________________

Add: ______________________

**3.** **A** vertebrate
**B** unfortunately
**C** tolerated

Family: ______________________

Add: ______________________

**4.** **A** mammal
**B** medical
**C** capital

Family: ______________________

Add: ______________________

**5.** **A** invertebrate
**B** incorrect
**C** inactive

Family: ______________________

Add: ______________________

**6.** **A** waterfall
**B** water buffalo
**C** watering can

Family: ______________________

Add: ______________________

**7.** **A** semiannual
**B** semisweet
**C** semifinal

Family: ______________________

Add: ______________________

**8.** **A** January
**B** primary
**C** stationary

Family: ______________________

Add: ______________________

Name ______________________________

## COMPARE AND CONTRAST

**Think about the similarities and differences between the words in each pair. Write a phrase or sentence to compare them, or tell how they are alike. Then write a phrase or sentence to contrast them, or tell how they are different.**

**1. crustacean, invertebrate**

Compare: ______________________________

Contrast: ______________________________

**2. arachnid, insect**

Compare: ______________________________

Contrast: ______________________________

**3. fish, amphibian**

Compare: ______________________________

Contrast: ______________________________

**4. salamander, lizard**

Compare: ______________________________

Contrast: ______________________________

**5. whale, elephant**

Compare: ______________________________

Contrast: ______________________________

**6. brown bat, owl**

Compare: ______________________________

Contrast: ______________________________

Name ______________________________

## RHYMING WORDS

**Turn the sentences and phrases below into rhymes by filling in each blank with a word from the Word Box.**

| relaxation | repose | recreation | pleasure |
|---|---|---|---|
| pastime | leisure | diversion | amusement |

1. **Example:** Take a rest from sneezing.

   ______Repose______ your nose.

2. There is no way to tell how much I enjoy soccer!

   You cannot measure my ______________!

3. An activity that is only done during July and August.

   a summertime ______________

4. A place set aside for those who need to unwind from a hard day.

   a ______________ station

5. Someone who likes to work all the time and does not want to be

   disturbed has an aversion to ______________.

6. The ballpark closed down and the team had to find somewhere else to play.

   This was a case of ______________ relocation.

7. I felt trapped inside all day by the heavy rains. My puppy thought it was a lot of fun having me at home all day.

   My imprisonment was my puppy's ______________.

8. These piano lessons have taken all my free time from me.

   I would call that a seizure of my ______________!

Name ____________________

## SYNONYMS

▶ **The words in the box are all related to recreation. Sort them into the diagram below according to their meaning.**

| | | | |
|---|---|---|---|
| **amusement** | **pastime** | **pleasure** | **recreation** |
| **diversion** | **leisure** | **repose** | **relaxation** |

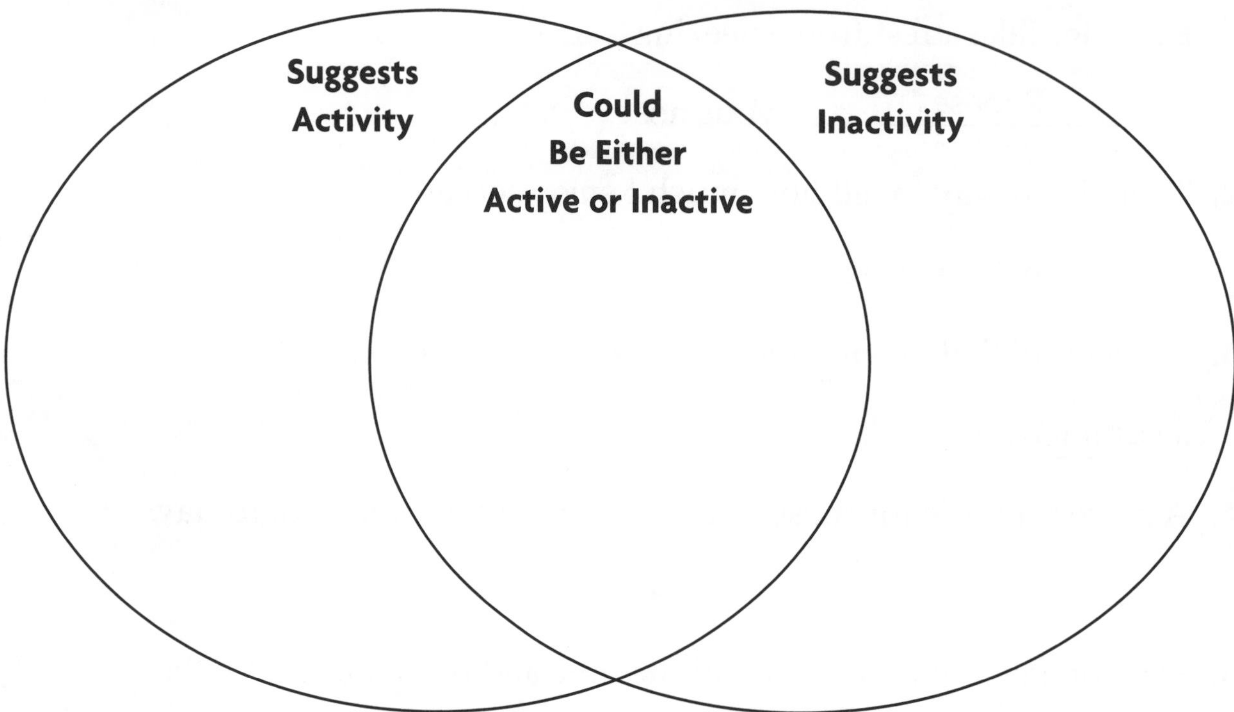


▶ **Now make a list of pastimes, or kinds of recreation, that are active and a list of pastimes that are not active.**

| **Active Pastimes** | **Inactive Pastimes** |
|---|---|
| ____________________ | ____________________ |
| ____________________ | ____________________ |
| ____________________ | ____________________ |
| ____________________ | ____________________ |
| ____________________ | ____________________ |
| ____________________ | ____________________ |

Name ___

## CONNOTATION/DENOTATION

▶ **Think about the meanings of the underlined words. Answer the questions with complete sentences.**

1. Would you prefer to do something for amusement or relaxation? Why?

___

___

2. Would you play soccer for pleasure or for repose? Explain.

___

___

3. Which is something you might make plans for, recreation or leisure? Explain why you think as you do.

___

___

4. Which do you take more seriously, a hobby or a pastime? Explain why you think as you do.

___

___

▶ **The following pairs have similar meanings. Circle the word that has a more positive connotation. Explain your choice.**

5. energetic aggressive

___

6. irritable excitable

___

7. uncivilized rugged

___

8. forgetful negligent

___

Name ____________________

## COMPARE AND CONTRAST

▶ **In the left column are names that tell about a person's level of experience or skill. Along the top are several features that may or may not apply to each label. Fill in each block as follows:**

**+ yes   – no   +/– maybe**

**Next, add two features of your own that apply to a few of the labels. Fill in each block as before.**

| | Paid | In training | Proficient | Experienced | Related to Sports | Related to Hobbies | | |
|---|---|---|---|---|---|---|---|---|
| amateur | | | | | | | | |
| beginner | | | | | | | | |
| dabbler | | | | | | | | |
| fledgling | | | | | | | | |
| novice | | | | | | | | |
| professional | | | | | | | | |
| rookie | | | | | | | | |
| trainee | | | | | | | | |
| expert | | | | | | | | |
| veteran | | | | | | | | |

▶ **Work with a partner to discuss and compare your completed charts.**

Name ____________________

## EUPHEMISMS

A **euphemism** is a word used instead of another word that may have an unpleasant connotation. Using a euphemism makes something sound nicer than it may really be.

▶ **In each pair below, the second sentence restates the first, using a euphemism. Complete each by replacing the underlined word(s) with a word from the box below. The first has been done for you.**

| **beginner** | **antique** | **fledgling** | **novice** |
|---|---|---|---|

1. You say: That skateboard is old and run-down.

   I reply: No, it's an antique.

2. You say: You're just a ____________ photographer.

   I reply: No. I'm an amateur, but I do have experience.

3. You say: You don't know what you're doing.

   I reply: I'm a ____________.

4. You say: A ____________ like Jim isn't good enough for our team.

   I reply: He's a rookie. I think you should give him a chance.

▶ **Now try this. One sentence is given to you. Write a second sentence using a euphemism for the underlined word or phrase. You may replace it with a word or a phrase. The first has been done for you.**

5. You say: I'm going to get drenched in that downpour!

   I reply: Oh, that's just a little drizzle.

6. You say: The paint on that sign has practically disappeared. I can't even read it.

   I reply: ____________________.

Name ______________________________

## ANTONYMS

**Choose antonym pairs from the box that match the pairs of definitions given.**

| | | | |
|---|---|---|---|
| **professional** | **rookie** | **dabbler** | **trainer** |
| **amateur** | **expert** | **trainee** | **veteran** |

**1.** paid ____________________

unpaid ____________________

**2.** enjoys something but doesn't take it seriously ____________________
studies carefully and has a lot of knowledge about something

____________________

**3.** has spent many years in this job ____________________

this is the first year in this job ____________________

**4.** is learning how to do a job ____________________

is teaching someone how to do a job ____________________

## COLLOQUIALISMS

A **colloquialism** is a way of saying something informally. For example, a *buck* is a colloquialism for a *dollar*.

**Match the colloquialism to the underlined word in each sentence.**

| | | |
|---|---|---|
| **pro** | **R & R** | **rookie** |

**1.** The police captain assigned an experienced officer to work with the recruit. ____________

**2.** Teresa hopes to be a professional golfer one day. ____________

**3.** Ed went to the beach for some rest and recreation. ____________

Name ____________________

## CLASSIFY/CATEGORIZE

**The words in the left column are all adjectives with similar meanings. Check the appropriate boxes to show how each word may be used. Then add some descriptive words of your own and check the boxes as before.**

| | Describes Language | Describes an Image | Describes a Person |
|---|---|---|---|
| vivid | | | |
| colorful | | | |
| descriptive | | | |
| emphatic | | | |
| radiant | | | |
| vibrant | | | |
| picturesque | | | |
| vivacious | | | |
| | | | |
| | | | |
| | | | |
| | | | |
| | | | |

Name ______________________________

## WORDS IN CONTEXT

**Think about the meaning of the underlined word. Then respond to each question or complete each sentence.**

1. A picturesque description would give readers or listeners a(n) ______________________________
______________________________.

2. The painting showed a radiant sunset behind the mountains. Describe what might make it seem *radiant*. ______________________________
______________________________.

3. Which of the following words might describe an emphatic speech?

assertive ____ soothing ____ demanding ____
timid ____ uncertain ____ powerful ____

4. Write five colorful words to describe a parade.
______________________________
______________________________.

5. Write five descriptive words to tell about a tree.
______________________________
______________________________.

6. Name three or more animals, plants, or things that have vibrant colors.
______________________________
______________________________.

7. Would you like to have a vivacious friend? Explain your reasons.
______________________________
______________________________.

Name ______________________________

## WORD LINES

**Arrange each group of words on a word line. Explain how you decided to arrange them. The first one is done for you.**

**1.** fast, quick, rapid, speedy, swift

quick, fast, speedy, swift, rapid

Each word expresses something a degree faster than the one before.

**2.** vivid, lifelike, descriptive, picturesque

______________________________

______________________________

**3.** brilliant, bright, radiant, colorful, vibrant

______________________________

______________________________

**4.** blast, boom, bang, roar, thunder

______________________________

______________________________

**5.** bit, crumb, dot, drop, grain

______________________________

______________________________

**6.** glad, happy, joyful, merry, cheerful

______________________________

______________________________

Name ____________________

## ANALOGIES

**An analogy is made of two pairs of words. The words in each pair are related in the same way. Think about the relationships in the following pairs of words. Then fill in the blank to complete the analogy.**

1. A *competition* is to a *competitor* as a *sculpture* is to a ____________.
2. A *rival* is to an *opponent* as a *victor* is to a ____________.
3. A *tournament* is to *athletic* as an *exhibition* is to ____________.
4. A *conflict* is to a *disagreement* as a ____________ is to a *competition.*
5. A *contender* is to a *title* as an *heir* is to a ____________.
6. A *finish line* is to a *race* as an ____________ is to a *book.*
7. *Lanes* are to a *swimming pool* as ____________ are to a *notebook.*
8. An *entry form* is to a *contest* as an ____________ is to a *job.*
9. A *trophy* is to a *prize* as a ____________ is to a *vegetable.*
10. *Champion* is to *championship* as *sportsman* is to ____________.

## RHYMING WORDS

**Think of another way to say the first sentence in each pair. Choose a word that rhymes with the underlined word.**

1. Due to rain, the match ended before a winner was decided.

   The ____________ was incomplete.
2. I'm pretty sure there's going to be an argument.

   I predict a ____________.
3. I waited for the girl I was competing against to get here.

   I waited for the arrival of my ____________.

Name ______________________________

## WORD FAMILIES

**Words can be related by a root or base word, or by word parts. In each group of words below, determine how the words are related. Then circle the letter of the word that is not related to the other three. The first has been done for you.**

**1.** **A** competition
**B** compromise
**C** compete
**D** competitor

Family: Base word *compete*

**2.** **A** contend
**B** contender
**C** contention
**D** competition

Family: ______________________

**3.** **A** opponent
**B** opposition
**C** oppose
**D** oppossum

Family: ______________________

**4.** **A** rival
**B** rivet
**C** rivalry
**D** rivalrous

Family: ______________________

**5.** **A** victory
**B** victor
**C** victorious
**D** victim

Family: ______________________

**6.** **A** torn
**B** tourist
**C** tournament
**D** tourmaline

Family: ______________________

**7.** **A** meet
**B** neatly
**C** fleet
**D** greeting

Family: ______________________

**8.** **A** conflict
**B** confusion
**C** contract
**D** counter

Family: ______________________

Name ______________________________

## CLASSIFY/CATEGORIZE

**Circle the letter of the word that doesn't belong in each list. Then name the category in the space provided.**

**1.** **A** contest
**B** meet
**C** tournament
**D** players

Name for category: ______________________________

**2.** **F** opponent
**G** contestant
**H** referee
**J** contender

Name for category: ______________________________

**3.** **A** tennis
**B** badminton
**C** volleyball
**D** cycling

Name for category: ______________________________

**4.** **F** infield
**G** goal line
**H** home plate
**J** pitcher's mound

Name for category: ______________________________

**5.** **A** batting helmet
**B** catcher's mask
**C** chest guard
**D** shoulder pads

Name for category: ______________________________

Name ______________________________

## ANALOGIES

▶ **Each pair of words in an analogy is related in the same way. Complete the following analogies.**

1. *Strength* is to *weakness* as *rapidly* is to ______________.

2. *Revitalize* is to *vigor* as *organize* is to ______________.

3. *Vitamin* is to *health* as ______________ is to *mathematics.*

4. *Vital* is to *essential* as *running shoes* are to ______________.

5. *Deficient* is to *supplement* as *thirsty* is to ______________.

6. *Lungs* are to *breathe* as *feet* are to ______________.

7. *Vitality* is to *weariness* as *confidence* is to ______________.

8. *Red* is to *tomato* as *green* is to ______________.

9. *Pears* are to ______________ as *broccoli* is to *spinach.*

10. *Wheat* is to ______________ as *milk* is to *dairy.*

▶ **Now try this. Complete each analogy by writing two pairs of words that are related in the same way. You may choose a word or words from the box, or write words of your own. The first one is started for you.**

| | | | |
|---|---|---|---|
| **round** | **orange** | **soccer** | **exercise** |
| **color** | **book** | **pastime** | **reading** |

11. Orange is to color as ______________ is to ______________.

12. ______________ is to ______________ as ______________ is to ______________.

13. ______________ is to ______________ as ______________ is to ______________.

14. ______________ is to ______________ as ______________ is to ______________.

Name ____________________

## LATIN ROOTS

**The words listed below come from the Latin word *vita,* which means "life." Read each definition. Then choose one of the words to complete each sentence below. Use the part of speech identified in the definitions as a clue for which word to choose.**

**revitalize** *verb* to give new life or energy to

**vitamin** *noun* a substance found in food and needed for the body's health and growth

**vital** *adjective* **1.** necessary to or supporting life **2.** very important or necessary

**vitality** *noun* **1.** vigor, energy **2.** the capacity to live, grow, and develop

**vitalize** *verb* **1.** to endow or provide with life **2.** to invigorate or animate

**vitals** *noun* those bodily organs whose functioning is essential to life

1. We get ____________ C from eating certain foods.
2. Healthy lungs are ____________ to life.
3. Three balanced meals a day help ensure a person's ____________.
4. Warm clothing is ____________ for a ski vacation.
5. The phrase "full of vim, vigor, and ____________" is often used to describe a person who is full of energy.
6. A person's ____________ include the brain, the heart, and the lungs.
7. A hearty breakfast will ____________ you for the day.
8. When you have been sitting still for a long time, exercise is a great way to ____________ the body.

Name ____________________

## CONTEXT CLUES

**Read the sentences below and circle the letter of the best definition of the underlined word. Use context to figure out the meaning of the word.**

1. Vitamins are <u>essential</u> to good health. They give you energy and keep you from getting sick.
   - **A** of great importance
   - **B** possibly helpful
   - **C** harmful
   - **D** of little importance

2. A medical test can show if you are vitamin-<u>deficient</u>. If you are, you may need to eat a lot of foods that are rich in vitamins.
   - **A** capable of doing a good job
   - **B** not easily achieved
   - **C** lacking the necessary amount
   - **D** put off until a later date

3. In addition to eating a healthful, balanced diet, some people also take a vitamin <u>supplement</u>. This gives them an extra dose of important vitamins.
   - **A** a kind of geometric angle
   - **B** something in addition to the main source
   - **C** something good you say about another person
   - **D** soft and bendable

4. Increased energy, or <u>vigor</u>, is the result of maintaining a balanced diet and of regular exercise.
   - **A** a feeling of weakness
   - **B** bodily strength
   - **C** electric current
   - **D** a type of exercise

5. After hiking for many hours, we swam in the cool lake and rested in the shade. We soon felt <u>revitalized</u> and ready to head back to camp.
   - **A** of importance to good health
   - **B** ready to go to sleep
   - **C** drained of energy; extremely tired
   - **D** renewed in energy or liveliness

Name ____________________

## WORD FAMILIES

**Words can be related by a root or base word. They may also be related by word parts. Read each group below and determine how the words are related. Cross out the one word that does not belong to that family, and then add another word that fits. The first has been done for you.**

**1.** **A** persistent
**B** persisting
**C** persevere
**D** persistence

Family: base word *persist*

Add: persist

**2.** **A** prevail
**B** present
**C** prepare
**D** person

Family: ____________________

Add: ____________________

**3.** **A** utterance
**B** prevail
**C** endurance
**D** perseverance

Family: ____________________

Add: ____________________

**4.** **A** strive
**B** live
**C** driver
**D** diva

Family: ____________________

Add: ____________________

**5.** **A** afloat
**B** perpetuate
**C** elongate
**D** grate

Family: ____________________

Add: ____________________

**6.** **A** evening
**B** endure
**C** encircle
**D** encyclopedia

Family: ____________________

Add: ____________________

**7.** **A** continue
**B** discontinue
**C** contain
**D** continual

Family: ____________________

Add: ____________________

**8.** **A** unwrap
**B** unpack
**C** under
**D** uncooked

Family: ____________________

Add: ____________________

Name ______________________________

## COMPARE AND CONTRAST

**Complete the following sentences to describe how the two items in italic type are alike or how they are different.**

1. A *tortoise* is like a *turtle* except that ______________________________

______________________________

2. *Perseverance* is like *persistence* except that ______________________________

______________________________

3. A *desert* is like a *beach* because ______________________________

______________________________

4. *To quit* is like *to surrender* except that ______________________________

______________________________

5. *To persist* is like *to strive* because ______________________________

______________________________

6. A *race* is like a *test* but ______________________________

______________________________

7. *Tiring* is like *exhausting* except that ______________________________

______________________________

8. *To endure* is like *to continue* but ______________________________

______________________________

9. A *folktale* is like a *legend* because ______________________________

______________________________

Name ______________________________________________

## CONTEXT CLUES

**Read each sentence, paying attention to the meaning of the underlined word. Write a definition for the word as it is used in the sentence.**

1. I strive to do my best at dance class, but I'm still not very good at it.

   *Strive* means ______________________________________________.

2. Hard work will prevail when all else fails.

   *Prevail* means ______________________________________________.

3. The cyclist could not endure the heat of the sun and rested until it became cooler.

   *Endure* means ______________________________________________.

4. We will perpetuate our traffic problems by continuing to buy more cars without expanding the roadways.

   *Perpetuate* means ______________________________________________.

5. Although learning a new language was difficult, I persevered, and now I can speak Spanish.

   *Persevered* means ______________________________________________.

6. John's persistence paid off. He found the baseball that his friends had thought was lost.

   *Persistence* means ______________________________________________.

7. The setting of the story was a desert in the southwestern United States.

   *Setting* means ______________________________________________.

8. Similar to a hare, a jackrabbit is a desert-dwelling animal with oversized ears that help it stay cool.

   A *jackrabbit* is ______________________________________________.

# Glossary

**a•bra•sion** [ə•brā′zhən] *n.* The process of wearing or rubbing something away: **Daily *abrasion* from shoes wore down the wooden floor.**

**a•cry•lic** [ə•kril′ik] *adj.* Made of or having to do with a special kind of plastic: **I prefer to use *acrylic* paint for outdoor scenes.**

**al•pine** [al′pīn] *adj.* Of, like, or located in mountains: **The *alpine* cottage is tucked between two mountains.**

**am•a•teur** [am′ə•chŏŏr] *n.* A person who performs an activity for enjoyment rather than for money: **The hero in the play at our community theater is an *amateur*.**

**am•bi•ance** [am′bē•əns] *n.* A surrounding atmosphere: **The artist's studio had a cheerful *ambiance*.**

**am•phib•i•an** [am•fib′ē•ən] *n.* An animal that can live both on land and in water: **The salamander, like every *amphibian*, is cold-blooded.**

**am•phib•i•ous** [am•fib′ē•əs] *adj.* Living or adapted to living on land or in water: **The swamp was full of *amphibious* plants.**

**a•muse•ment** [ə•myōōz′mənt] *n.* The condition of being entertained; enjoyment: **The children shared hours of *amusement* during their visit to the zoo.**

**a•nat•o•my** [ə•nat′ə•mē] *n.* The scientific study of the structure of plants or animals: **Brianna will study *anatomy* next year.**

**an•ces•tor** [an′ses•tər] *n.* A person from whom one is descended: **My *ancestor* sailed from France to Louisiana in the 1850s.**

**ap•prox•i•mate•ly** [ə•prok′sə•mit•lē] *adv.* Close to; about: **Our city got *approximately* 5 inches of rain last month.**

**a•quat•ic** [ə•kwät′ik] *adj.* Living or growing in or on water: **Water lilies are an *aquatic* plant.**

**a•que•duct** [ak′wə•dukt′] *n.* An artificial channel for carrying water: **We learned about an ancient *aqueduct* in Rome.**

**a•rach•nid** [ə•rak′nid] *n.* Any of a class of animals with four pairs of legs but no antennae or wings: **My dad doesn't like spiders or any other *arachnid*.**

**ar•bor•e•tum** [är′bə•rē′təm] *n.* A place where trees and shrubs are grown for study: **The *arboretum* has unusual plants from Asia.**

**arc•tic** [är(k)′tik] *adj.* Of or having to do with the region of the North Pole: **Researchers must wear heavy coats to protect themselves against the *arctic* wind.**

**ar•id** [ar′id] *adj.* Without enough rainfall to grow things; dry: **The Sahara is one of the most *arid* regions on earth.**

**ar•range•ment** [ə•rānj′mənt] *n.* The way in which something is ordered: **The art teacher fussed over the *arrangement* of the new paintings.**

**arts** [ärts] *n., pl.* Fields of study that include literature, philosophy, and languages, but not the sciences: **Study of the *arts* is essential to a balanced education.**

**as•ter** [as′tər] *n.* A plant with flowers like daisies: **The *aster* growing in my garden has purple petals.**

**as•ter•isk** [as′tər•isk] *n.* A mark shaped like a star (*) used to show a note is provided: **The *asterisk* in the text reminded me to look at the footnote.**

**as•ter•oid** [as′tə•roid] *n.* Any of thousands of tiny planets orbiting the sun between Mars and Jupiter: **Ceres, the first known *asteroid*, was discovered in 1801.**

| | | | | | | |
|---|---|---|---|---|---|---|
| a add | e end | o odd | ōō pool | oi oil | th this | ə = *a* in *above* |
| ā ace | ē equal | ō open | u up | ou pout | zh vision | *e* in *sicken* |
| â care | i it | ô order | û burn | ng ring | | *i* in *possible* |
| ä palm | ī ice | ŏŏ took | yōō fuse | th thin | | *o* in *melon* |
| | | | | | | *u* in *circus* |

**as•tral** [as′trəl] *adj.* Of or relating to the stars: **The observatory made nightly *astral* observations.**

**as•tro•dome** [as′trə•dōm′] *n.* A transparent dome on the top of an aircraft: **The navigator checked the position of the stars through the *astrodome*.**

**as•tro•naut** [as′trə•nôt′] *n.* A person who is trained to travel in or fly a spacecraft: **The *astronaut* will attempt a space walk.**

**as•tro•nau•tics** [as′trə•nô′tiks] *n.* The science of flight in space: **Specialists in *astronautics* will design parts for the space shuttle.**

**as•tron•o•mer** [ə•stron′ə•mər] *n.* A person who studies stars, planets, and other space objects: **Johannes Kepler, a German *astronomer*, discovered that the planets follow oval-shaped orbits.**

**at•mos•phere** [at′məs•fir] *n.* The air surrounding the earth: **The *atmosphere* is made of mostly nitrogen and oxygen.**

**auc•tion•eer** [ôk′shən•ir′] *n.* A person who conducts an auction (a public sale): **The *auctioneer* kept the sale moving.**

**au•di•to•ry** [ô′də•tôr′ē] *adj.* Of or having to do with hearing: **The *auditory* nerves connect the inner ear to the brain.**

**au•to•bi•og•ra•phy** [ô′tə•bī•og′rə•fē] *n.* The story of a person's life written by that person: **The famous dancer wrote her *autobiography*.**

**au•to•graph** [ô′tə•graf′] *n.* A person's own signature: **I waited at the arena to get my favorite star's *autograph*.**

## B

**bare•ly** [bâr′lē] *adv.* Only just; scarcely: **We have *barely* enough snow for a snowman.**

**be•gin•ner** [bi•gin′ər] *n.* A person who has little experience or is doing something for the first time: **Every *beginner* at the piano recital was nervous.**

**bi•og•ra•phy** [bī•og′rə•fē] *n.* The story of a person's life and experiences: **Juanita read a *biography* of Thomas Jefferson before writing her report.**

**blos•som** [blos′əm] *v.* To develop or grow; flourish: **The young dancers will *blossom* under the famous ballerina's teaching.**

**bo•tan•i•cal** [bə•tan′i•kəl] *adj.* Having to do with plants or with botany: **The *botanical* show attracts thousands of gardeners each spring.**

**bot•an•ist** [bot′ən•ist] *n.* A scientist who studies plants and plant life: **The *botanist* closely examined the needles of the cactus.**

**bot•a•ny** [bot′ə•nē] *n.* The study of plants: **Madison has decided to study *botany* instead of zoology.**

**boul•e•vard** [bo͝ol′ə•värd′] *n.* A broad city street or main road, often lined with trees: **The parade ran the entire length of the *boulevard*.**

**bris•tle** [bris′(ə)l] *n.* Coarse, stiff hair, often used for brushes: **I cleaned the *bristles* of the brush after I finished painting.**

**budg•et** [buj′it] *n.* A plan for spending money over a period of time: **I will save money if I stay within my *budget*.**

**busi•ness** [biz′nis] *n.* A commercial or industrial enterprise: **The only *business* on Main Street is a clothing store.**

## C

**ca•nal** [kə•nal′] *n.* A waterway constructed across land: **A *canal* is often an important shipping route.**

**can•vas** [kan′vəs] *n.* A cloth surface specially prepared for a painter to use: **The artist dabbed paint onto the *canvas*.**

**car•ni•val** [kär′nə•vəl] *n.* An amusement show, typically with rides and shows: **This year's *carnival* will have a Ferris wheel.**

**car•ou•sel** [kar′ə•sel′] *n.* A merry-go-round: **The children enjoyed riding the *carousel.***

**chance** [chans] *n.* A possibility or opportunity: **Give him another *chance* to succeed.**

**cho•re•o•graph** [kôr′ē•ə•graf′] *v.* To make up combinations of steps to create a dance: **I want to *choreograph* my own performance.**

**cho•re•og•ra•pher** [kôr′ē•og′rə•fər] *n.* A person who creates dance movements: **The *choreographer* explained what the dancers were to do.**

**cir•cum•stance** [sûr′kəm•stans′] *n.* A condition: **Ice on the roads is a *circumstance* that may cause traffic accidents.**

**civ•ic** [siv′ik] *adj.* Of or having to do with a city: **The mayor asked the citizens to do their *civic* duty and vote.**

**civ•i•li•za•tion** [siv′ə•lə•zā′shən] *n.* The society and culture of a particular people, place, or period: **Archaeological remains in South America provide important information about the Inca *civilization.***

**cli•mate** [klī′mit] *n.* The kind of weather a place has over a period of time: **Tropical islands often have a pleasant *climate.***

**coast•al** [kōs′təl] *adj.* Of, on, or near the coast: **Charleston, South Carolina, is a *coastal* city.**

**coast•line** [kōst′līn′] *n.* The outline or border of a coast: **The *coastline* of New England is beautiful on sunny days.**

**col•or•ful** [kul′ər•fəl] *adj.* Full of bright colors: **The leaves are *colorful* in autumn.**

**com•pe•ti•tion** [kom•pə•tish′ən] *n.* A contest: **Diane is an excellent artist, and she usually wins the annual watercolor *competition* at the museum.**

**com•pose** [kəm•pōz′] *v.* To create: **Mr. Gonzalez will *compose* a letter to the school board.**

**com•po•si•tion** [kom′pə•zish′ən] *n.* The parts that make up something: **Our science teacher explained the *composition* of the air we breathe.**

**con•duct** [kən•dukt′] *v.* To lead a musical group: **Mr. Saunders will *conduct* the orchestra on Sunday.**

**con•duc•tor** [kən•duk′tər] *n.* A person who leads or guides, usually for an orchestra or chorus: **The orchestra members watched the *conductor* for the cue to begin playing.**

**con•flict** [kon′flikt] *n.* A struggle, fight, or battle: **Several nations sent troops to help end the *conflict.***

**con•ten•der** [kən•ten′dər] *n.* A person who participates in a competition: **The senator is a *contender* for the presidential nomination.**

**con•tin•u•ous** [kən•tin′yo͞o•əs] *adj.* Going on without any pause or interruption: **Our homes and schools need a *continuous* supply of electricity.**

**cred•it** [kred′it] *n.* Any deposit or sum of money against which a person may draw: **I received store *credit* for the sweater that I returned.**

| | | | | | | |
|---|---|---|---|---|---|---|
| a add | e end | o odd | o͞o pool | oi oil | th this | ə = *a* in *above* |
| ā ace | ē equal | ō open | u up | ou pout | zh vision | *e* in *sicken* |
| â care | i it | ô order | û burn | ng ring | | *i* in *possible* |
| ä palm | ī ice | o͝o took | yo͞o fuse | th thin | | *o* in *melon* |
| | | | | | | *u* in *circus* |

**crus•ta•cean** [krus•tā′shən] *n.* An animal, such as a lobster or crab, with a tough outer shell and a segmented body that lives in water: **The largest *crustacean* is the giant spider crab.**

**cui•sine** [kwi•zēn′] *n.* A style or type of cooking: **I like Mexican *cuisine,* but my sister likes Japanese *cuisine.***

**cul•ture** [kul′chər] *n.* The ideas and way of life of a group of people at a particular time. Culture includes language, customs, music, art, food, and games. **In North American *culture,* people shake hands when they meet.**

**cur•ren•cy** [kûr′ən•sē] *n.* Money in general use that is available for exchange: **I will exchange my American dollars for Mexican *currency* before I leave.**

**dab•bler** [dab′lər] *n.* Someone who does something, but not very seriously: **Nathan is a serious painter, but I'm only a *dabbler* in art.**

**debt** [det] *n.* An amount that a person owes to another: **Letisha owes Kim a *debt* of five dollars.**

**ded•i•ca•tion** [ded′ə•kā′shən] *n.* The act of setting apart for or devoting to a special purpose: **The mayor and governor attended the *dedication* of the park.**

**de•fi•ci•ent** [di•fish′ənt] *adj.* Not complete: **His understanding of fractions is *deficient.***

**del•ta** [del′tə] *n.* The flat plain at a river's mouth made of soil that the river has carried downstream: **The Nile River creates a vast *delta* in northern Egypt.**

**de•mol•ish** [di•mol′ish] *v.* To tear down completely; destroy: **The bulldozer will *demolish* the abandoned house.**

**de•scrip•tive** [di•skrip′tiv] *adj.* Telling what a person or thing is like: **The magazine is full of *descriptive* articles about towns in Texas.**

**de•stroy** [di•stroi′] *v.* To ruin completely: **One tornado can *destroy* a neighborhood.**

**dev•as•tate** [dev′ə•stāt] *v.* To leave in ruins; destroy: **The approaching hurricane is likely to *devastate* the island.**

**di•a•ry** [dī′(ə•)rē] *n.* A book or journal in which one writes about personal events, experiences, and thoughts: **I like to write in my *diary* before I go to sleep at night.**

**di•ur•nal** [di•ûrn′əl] *adj.* Of or happening during the day: ***Diurnal* animals are awake during the day and asleep at night.**

**di•ver•sion** [di•vûr′zhən] *n.* An amusement, game, or pastime done for relaxation or distraction: **The crossword puzzle was a pleasant *diversion* on the long car trip.**

**down•town** [doun′toun′] *adv.* In the main business district of a town or city: **When you are *downtown,* you can take the subway or the bus.**

**drench** [drench] *v.* To wet thoroughly; soak: **If we don't find an umbrella, the rain will *drench* us.**

**ea•sel** [ē′zəl] *n.* A frame on legs used to hold canvas or paper for painting, a chart, or other items: **Our teacher placed the map on an *easel.***

**e•con•o•my** [i•kä′nə•mē] *n.* The system of earning and managing money or resources in a family, business, or community of any size: **The national *economy* is strong.**

**em•pha•tic** [em•fat′ik] *adj.* Done or spoken with forceful speech: **Our mother was *emphatic* about our cleaning the playroom.**

**em•ploy•ment** [im•ploi′mənt] *n.* A job or

occupation: **She found *employment* at the bank.**

**en•dure** [in•d(y)ŏŏr′] *v.* To put up with; bear; tolerate: **Athletes must sometimes *endure* pain during an event.**

**en•gi•neer** [en′jə•nir′] *n.* A person who is trained in the skill of putting scientific knowledge to practical use, as in the construction of roads, bridges, and machinery: **The city hired an *engineer* to plan the new highway.**

**en•ter•tain** [en•tər•tān′] *v.* To hold the attention of and give enjoyment to: **Our dog, Buddy, can *entertain* the neighborhood children for hours.**

**e•ro•sion** [i•rō′zhən] *n.* The gradual wearing away of soil or rock by water or wind: **The powerful waves from the storm caused severe *erosion* of the beach.**

**es•sen•tial** [i•sen′shəl] *adj.* Extremely important or necessary; vital: **It is *essential* that you unplug the iron when you finish using it.**

**eth•ni•ci•ty** [eth•nis′ət•ē] *n.* The characteristics of a particular group, such as race, country of origin, religion, or culture: **The *ethnicity* of the neighborhood is mixed.**

**ex•act•ly** [ig•zakt′lē] *adv.* Precisely; just so: **The train ride lasted *exactly* fifteen minutes.**

**ex•tra-sen•si•tive** [ek′strə-sen′sə•tiv] *adj.* Especially capable of feeling or reacting quickly or easily: **My uncle is *extra-sensitive* about his nickname.**

**ex•traor•din•ary** [ik•strôr′də•ner′ē *or* ek′strə•ôr′də•ner′ē] *adj.* Remarkable; unusual; surprising: **The fireworks on Independence Day were *extraordinary*.**

**fa•ble** [fā′bəl] *n.* A short story that teaches a lesson, often using animals as characters: **My sister's favorite *fable* is "The Crow and the Pitcher."**

**fic•tion** [fik′shən] *n.* A form of literature whose characters and events are entirely or partly imaginary: **The author's newest story is a work of *fiction*.**

**fledg•ling** [flej′ling] *n.* A young, inexperienced person; beginner: **Unlike the older violinists, I am only a *fledgling*.**

**flo•ra** [flôr′ə] *n.* All the plants of a particular place or period of time: **The *flora* of Florida includes many kinds of palm trees.**

**flour•ish** [flûr′ish] *v.* To grow vigorously; thrive: **Many different plants can *flourish* on tropical islands.**

**flow•er** [flou′ər] *n.* The part of a plant or tree that encloses the seeds; blossom: **The *flower* on this plant has bright yellow petals.**

**fo•li•age** [fō′lē•ij or fō′lij] *n.* The leaves on a tree or other plant: **The *foliage* on this plant comes out after the flowers do.**

**folk•lore** [fōk′lôr′] *n.* The beliefs, stories, and customs preserved among a people: **Paul Bunyan is a popular character in American *folklore*.**

**folk•tale** [fōk′tāl′] *n.* A traditional story handed down by word of mouth: **The story of Johnny Appleseed is an American *folktale*.**

**form** [fôrm] *n.* A mold, frame, or model that gives shape to something: **The toy company made a *form* to produce a new doll.**

| | | | | | | | | | | | | | |
|---|---|---|---|---|---|---|---|---|---|---|---|---|---|
| a | add | e | end | o | odd | o͞o | pool | oi | oil | th | this | ə = | *a* in *above* |
| ā | ace | ē | equal | ō | open | u | up | ou | pout | zh | vision | | *e* in *sicken* |
| â | care | i | it | ô | order | û | burn | ng | ring | | | | *i* in *possible* |
| ä | palm | ī | ice | ŏŏ | took | yo͞o | fuse | th | thin | | | | *o* in *melon* |
| | | | | | | | | | | | | | *u* in *circus* |

**frame** [frām] *n.* A basic inner structure that gives support and shape to the thing built around it: **The skyscraper's *frame* is made of steel.**

**frame•work** [frām′wûrk′] *n.* The basic inner structure around which a thing is built: **Our cabin has a wooden *framework*.**

**ge•ne•al•o•gy** [jē′nē•al′ə•jē *or* jē′nē•ol′ə•jē] *n.* A record of the ancestors and descent of a person or family: **Aunt Lucy is the expert on our family's *genealogy*.**

**ge•og•ra•pher** [jē•og′rə•fər] *n.* A person who studies the features of the earth's surface: **The small island was mapped by a *geographer*.**

**ge•ol•o•gist** [jē•ol′ə•jist] *n.* A scientist who studies the history and structure of the earth: **A *geologist* visited our class and explained the history of several rocks.**

**gild•ed** [gil′dəd] *v.* Covered or coated with a thin layer of gold: **He *gilded* the front of the picture frame.**

**gla•cier** [glā′shər] *n.* A large mass of ice that moves very slowly: **An immense *glacier* covers much of Antarctica.**

**grav•el** [grav′əl] *n.* A mixture of small pebbles and pieces of rock: **It is difficult to ride our bikes on *gravel*.**

**grav•i•ty** [grav′ə•tē] *n.* The pull of stars, planets, and moons on objects near them: **Astronauts are weightless in space because they are beyond earth's *gravity*.**

**green•house** [grēn′hous′] *n.* A heated building, usually made of glass, that is used for growing plants: **We can grow flowers in the *greenhouse* during the winter.**

**hab•i•tat** [hab′ə•tat] *n.* The place where an animal or plant naturally lives or grows: **The *habitat* of goldfish is fresh water.**

**hap•pen•stance** [hap′ən•stans′] *n.* A chance occurrence: **It was just *happenstance* that we met in the park.**

**he•red•i•ty** [hə•red′ə•tē] *n.* The passing on of characteristics from parents to children by means of genes: **My hair is blond and my eyes are brown because of *heredity*.**

**her•i•tage** [her′ə•tij] *n.* Traditions or customs handed down from one generation to the next: **Texas has a *heritage* of pride and independence.**

**his•to•ry** [his′tə•rē] *n.* Past events, or a record of them, often concerning a particular nation, people, or activity: **Our class is studying the *history* of the United States.**

**hy•drate** [hī′drāt] *v.* To cause to take up water: **Drink plenty of fluids to *hydrate* yourself before, during, and after exercise.**

**im•pres•sion** [im•presh′ən] *n.* Any mark made by pressing: **My shoes made an *impression* in the thick carpet.**

**in•ac•cu•rate•ly** [in•ak′yər•it•lē] *adv.* Incorrectly: **The news team *inaccurately* reported the time and place of the robbery.**

**in•her•i•tance** [in•her′ə•təns] *n.* Something obtained from someone upon his or her death, by will or law: **Mrs. Lopez received an antique watch as an *inheritance*.**

**in•let** [in′let′ *or* in′lət] *n.* A narrow strip of water leading inland from a larger body of water: **The boats are kept in the *inlet*, where the water is calmer.**

**in•ter•view** [in′tər•vyo͞o] *n.* A meeting between two or more people for the purpose of obtaining information: **A reporter will have an *interview* with the**

mayor to find out about the new city library.**

**in•ver•te•brate** [in•vûr′tə•brit *or* in•vûr′tə•brāt′] *n.* An animal without a backbone: **An ant is an *invertebrate*.**

**ir•ri•gate** [ir′ə•gāt′] *v.* To bring water to land by using pipes, ditches, or canals: **The farmers *irrigate* their crops by pumping water from the nearby lake.**

**jew•el•er** [jo͞o′əl•ər *or* jo͞o′lər] *n.* A person who sells, repairs, or makes jewelry: **The *jeweler* showed wedding rings to the couple.**

**jour•nal** [jûr′nəl] *n.* A daily account of events or thoughts: **I wrote in my *journal* every day I was at camp.**

**land•scape** [land′skāp′] *n.* A stretch of natural scenery on land as seen from a single point: **From the top of the mountain, you can see the *landscape* of the whole park.**

**lan•guage** [lang′gwij] *n.* The words that a certain nation or group uses in speaking and writing: **English is an official *language* of South Africa.**

**leg•a•cy** [leg′ə•sē] *n.* Money or property that has been left to one by a will: **His aunt left him a generous *legacy* when she died.**

**lei•sure** [lē′zhər or lezh′ər] *n.* Time free from work, study, or other duties: **During summer vacation, Tyrone has the *leisure* to skate with his friends.**

**lit•er•a•ture** [lit′ər•ə•chûr] *n.* Written works that show imagination and artistic skill: **The author has won many awards for her contributions to children's *literature*.**

**live•li•hood** [līv′lē•ho͝od′] *n.* The means by which one supports one's life: **How do you earn your *livelihood*?**

**mag•ma** [mag′mə] *n.* The hot, partly liquid mass of rock within the earth: **When *magma* moves to the surface of the earth, it becomes lava.**

**mam•mal** [mam′əl] *n.* Any vertebrate animal the females of which produce milk to feed their offspring: **The blue whale, the largest living animal, is a *mammal*.**

**ma•rine** [mə•rēn′] *adj.* Having to do with, formed by, or found in the sea: **Some *marine* animals live deep below the surface of the ocean.**

**mar•i•ner** [mar′ə•nər] *n.* A sailor: **The *mariner* raised the sails of his small boat.**

**mar•i•time** [mar′ə•tīm′] *adj.* Of or having to do with the sea: **Captains of ships must be familiar with *maritime* laws.**

**me•an•der** [mē•an′dər] *v.* To wind or turn, as a path or river: **The streams *meander* through the forest.**

**meet** [mēt] *n.* An assembly or gathering, as for a sports event: **Tomorrow I have a track *meet*.**

**me•lo•di•ous** [mə•lō′dē•əs] *adj.* Pleasant to hear; musical: **The singer has a *melodious* voice.**

**mem•oir** [mem′wär] *n.* The story of a person's own life and experiences: **Presidents sometimes write a *memoir* about their time in office.**

**met•ro•pol•i•tan** [met′rə•pol′ə•tən] *adj.* Of or having to do with a large city: **The

| | | | | | | |
|---|---|---|---|---|---|---|
| a add | e end | o odd | o͞o pool | oi oil | th this | ə = *a* in *above* |
| ā ace | ē equal | ō open | u up | ou pout | zh vision | *e* in *sicken* |
| â care | i it | ô order | û burn | ng ring | | *i* in *possible* |
| ä palm | ī ice | o͝o took | yo͞o fuse | th thin | | *o* in *melon* |
| | | | | | | *u* in *circus* |

***metropolitan* area has many old neighborhoods.**

**mois•ten** [mois′ən] *v.* To make slightly wet or damp: **Please *moisten* the stamp and place it on the envelope.**

**mold** [mōld] *n.* A hollow form that gives a particular shape to something soft or liquid: **The toy figures are made by pouring hot plastic into a *mold*.**

**mon•u•ment** [mon′yə•ment] *n.* Something, such as a building, statue, or arch, built in memory of a person or event: **The Jefferson Memorial is a *monument* in Washington, D.C.**

**moun•tain•eer** [moun′tən•ir′] *n.* A mountain climber: **Aaron, who is a *mountaineer*, has climbed Mount Rainier twice.**

**mu•ni•ci•pal** [myo͞o•nis′ə•pəl] *adj.* Of or having to do with a town or city or its local government: **There are three *municipal* parking garages downtown.**

**mu•si•cal** [myo͞o′zi•kəl] *adj.* Of, having to do with, or related to music: **Do you play a *musical* instrument?**

**myth** [mith] *n.* A traditional story, often offering an explanation of something in nature or of past events: **I read a *myth* about why the snow leopard is white.**

**nar•ra•tive** [nar′ə•tiv] *n.* An account, story, or tale: **The detectives asked the suspects for a *narrative* of their activities on the day of the robbery.**

**nau•ti•cal** [nô′ti•kəl] *adj.* Of or having to do with ships, sailors, or the sea: **The admiral looked closely at a *nautical* map as he plotted the fleet's next move.**

**na•val** [nā′vəl] *adj.* Of, for, done by, or having to do with the navy: **An ensign is the lowest ranking *naval* officer.**

**near•ly** [nir′lē] *adv.* Almost; practically; close to: **It is *nearly* time for lunch.**

**noc•tur•nal** [nok•tûr′nəl] *adj.* Of or happening at night: **The campers were not afraid of the *nocturnal* sounds.**

**non•fic•tion** [non′fik′shən] *adj.* Writing that is true and does not contain imaginary events or characters: **The magazine contains *nonfiction* articles as well as creative stories.**

**nov•ice** [nov′is] *n.* A beginner or inexperienced person: **Eric is still a *novice* at basketball, but he is learning quickly.**

**o•a•sis** [ō•ā′sis] *n.* An area in the desert made fertile by a water supply: **In contrast to the barren desert, the *oasis* had palm trees and green bushes.**

**ob•lit•er•ate** [ə•blit′ə•rāt′] *v.* To destroy completely: **Elise watched the fire *obliterate* an old shed.**

**oc•ca•sion** [ə•kā′zhən] *n.* An important event: **All of my friends were with me for the happy *occasion*.**

**oc•cu•pa•tion** [ok′yə•pā′shən] *n.* The work by which a person earns a living: **Her *occupation* is newspaper reporter.**

**oc•cur•rence** [ə•kûr′əns] *n.* The act or fact of something happening or taking place: **The unexpected *occurrence* of the disease worried the doctors.**

**o•ce•an•ic** [ō′shē•an′ik] *adj.* Of, living in, or produced by the ocean: **The ship will be the scientists' *oceanic* home for a month.**

**oc•u•lar** [ok′yə•lər] *adj.* Of, having to do with, or like the eye: **After giving me an *ocular* exam, the optometrist fitted me for eyeglasses.**

**ol•fac•to•ry** [ol•fak′tər•ē] *adj.* Of or having to do with the sense of smell: **People with**

a poor sense of taste may have a limited *olfactory* sense as well.

**op•po•nent** [ə•pō′nənt] *n.* A person who takes the opposite side in a fight, game, or contest: **She faced her *opponent* on the other soccer team.**

**op•por•tu•ni•ty** [op′ər•tyōō′nə•tē] *n.* A right or convenient time, occasion, or circumstance: **I had the *opportunity* to visit a national park this summer.**

**or•ches•trate** [ôr′kəs•trāt′] *v.* To arrange music for an orchestra: **A professional composer will *orchestrate* our winter musical.**

**or•der** [ôr′dər] *n.* A special or particular arrangement of things one after the other: **Put these words in alphabetical *order*.**

**or•gan•i•za•tion** [ôr′gən•ə•zā′shən] *n.* The act or condition of being in good order: **The *organization* of my desk helps me find things easily.**

**or•i•gin** [ôr′ə•jin] *n.* The beginning of the existence of anything: **The *origin* of that story is unknown.**

**or•nate** [ôr•nāt′] *adj.* Fancy or showy: **The house had an *ornate* mirror hanging in the hall.**

**ox•y•gen** [ok′sə•jin] *n.* A colorless, tasteless, odorless gas: **One-fifth of the earth's atmosphere is *oxygen*.**

**o•zone** [ō′zōn′] *adj.* An unstable form of oxygen that has a sharp odor: ***Ozone* is found naturally in earth's upper atmosphere.**

**pal•ette** [pal′it] *n.* A board used by an artist for mixing and holding paints: **The artist's *palette* held a rainbow of colorful oil paints.**

**pas•time** [pas′tīm′] *n.* Something that makes time pass pleasantly, as a sport or hobby: **Stephen's favorite *pastime* is reading.**

**ped•es•tal** [ped′is•təl] *n.* The base that supports a column, a statue, or a vase: **I accidentally bumped the *pedestal*, and the vase toppled to the floor.**

**pe•des•tri•an** [pə•dəs′trē•ən] *n.* A person who travels on foot: **A *pedestrian* could easily fall into that hole in the sidewalk.**

**per•cep•tion** [pər•sep′shən] *n.* The ability to become aware of things by means of senses: **My visual *perception* was not very good in the dark room.**

**per•form** [pər•fôrm′] *v.* To give an exhibition of artistic skill before an audience: **The choir will *perform* for the whole school.**

**per•pet•u•ate** [pər•pech′ōō•āt′] *v.* To cause to last a very long time: **He left money in his will to *perpetuate* the good deeds he had done for the community.**

**per•se•ver•ance** [pûr′sə•vir′əns] *n.* The continuing attempt to do something in spite of difficulties: **With much *perseverance*, she was able to finish the race.**

**per•se•vere** [pûr•sə•vîr′] *v.* To keep trying in spite of difficulties: **My science teacher encouraged me to *persevere* in my study of space.**

**per•sist** [pər•sist′] *v.* To continue firmly in spite of opposition, warning, or difficulty: **Jen and Karen *persist* in their batting practice, hoping to hit home runs.**

**per•sis•tence** [pər•sis′təns] *n.* The act of continuing firmly in spite of opposition, warning, or difficulty: **Her *persistence* and**

| | | | | | | | | | | | |
|---|---|---|---|---|---|---|---|---|---|---|---|
| a | add | e | end | o | odd | ōō | pool | oi | oil | th | this |
| ā | ace | ē | equal | ō | open | u | up | ou | pout | zh | vision |
| â | care | i | it | ô | order | û | burn | ng | ring | | |
| ä | palm | ī | ice | ŏŏ | took | yōō | fuse | th | thin | | |

ə = *a* in *above*, *e* in *sicken*, *i* in *possible*, *o* in *melon*, *u* in *circus*

**positive attitude helped her achieve her goal.**

**pe•tro•le•um** [pə•trō′lē•əm] *n.* A dark, thick, oily liquid found in the earth and used to make fuels: **Gasoline is made from *petroleum*.**

**pho•to•graph** [fō′tə•graf′] *n.* A picture made with a camera: **My grandmother has a *photograph* of her mother as a young girl.**

**pho•tog•ra•pher** [fə•tog′rə•fər] *n.* A person who takes pictures with a camera: **The *photographer* took pictures of everyone at the wedding.**

**pic•tur•esque** [pik′chə•resk′] *adj.* Having the kind of beauty suitable for a painted picture: **The village, nestled in the valley beside an orchard, is quite *picturesque*.**

**pi•o•neer** [pī′ə•nir′] *n.* Someone who leads the way, as in developing a new field: **He was a *pioneer* in computer engineering.**

**plaque** [plak] *n.* A metal, wood, or stone plate with writing on it attached to a wall or object to identify a person, place, or event: **Tourists were reading the *plaque* on a statue.**

**plea•sure** [plezh′ər] *n.* A feeling of enjoyment, delight, or satisfaction: **My cats give me great *pleasure*.**

**po•di•a•trist** [pə•dī′ə•trəst] *n.* A doctor who treats injuries and other problems related to feet: **I visited a *podiatrist* when I had an ingrown toenail.**

**po•e•try** [pō′ə•trē] *n.* The art of writing poems: ***Poetry* has been popular since ancient times.**

**po•si•tion** [pə•zish′ən] *n.* A job; employment: **She has an excellent *position* as principal of a school.**

**pre•cise•ly** [pri•sīs′lē] *adv.* Accurately; exactly: **Can you tell us *precisely* when the train will arrive?**

**pre•vail** [pri•vāl′] *v.* To gain control; be victorious: **We hope our soccer team will *prevail* in the championship match.**

**pro•ba•bil•ity** [prob′ə•bil′ə•tē] *n.* The likelihood of something happening: **The *probability* that it will snow today is low.**

**pro•fes•sion** [prə•fesh′ən] *n.* A field of work that requires thinking rather than physical labor: **There are many different careers to choose from in the medical *profession*.**

**pro•fes•sion•al** [prə•fesh′ən•əl] *adj.* Working for money in a field often entered by amateurs: **She is a *professional* athlete.**

**pro•gress** [prə•gres′] *v.* To advance toward a goal; develop; improve: **Our teachers expect us to *progress* quickly in our study of history.**

**pro•gres•sion** [prə•gresh′ən] *n.* A series or sequence, as of events: **A *progression* of events led to our move to Dallas.**

**pros•per** [pros′pər] *v.* To be successful; thrive: **Our town will *prosper* when the new factories open.**

**pur•suit** [pər•s(y)o͞ot′] *n.* An activity that is regularly done or followed, as a profession, hobby, or sport: **Scuba diving is a thrilling and fascinating *pursuit*.**

**ra•di•ant** [rā′dē•ənt] *adj.* Very bright and shining; brilliant: **The *radiant* sun reflected off the snow.**

**rec•re•a•tion** [rek′rē•ā′shən] *n.* An enjoyable activity or other form of amusement, relaxation, or play: **My sister and I play tennis for *recreation*.**

**re•fur•bish** [rē•fûr′bish] *v.* To brighten or freshen up; redecorate or renovate: **My parents will *refurbish* the apartment before we move in.**

**re•lax•a•tion** [rē′lak•sā′shən] *n.* The act of resting from work or exercise: **For *relaxation*, he read a book beside the pool.**

**ren•o•vate** [ren′ə•vāt′] *v.* To make something look like new; freshen; repair: **The school will *renovate* our media center during the summer.**

**re•pose** [ri•pōz′] *n.* Rest or sleep: **The artist painted a woman in contented *repose*.**

**rep•til•i•an** [rep•til′ē•ən] *adj.* Of, having to do with, or characteristic of a reptile: **We found a nest of *reptilian* eggs beside the pond.**

**re•sour•ces** [ri•sor′sez *or* rē′sôr′səz] *n., pl.* A supply of something that can be used or drawn on: **They had the cash *resources* to buy a new car.**

**re•store** [ri•stôr′] *v.* To bring back to a former or original condition: **Polishing will help *restore* the wooden desk.**

**re•vi•ta•lize** [rē•vīt′əl•īz′] *v.* To give new life or energy to something: **Another win will *revitalize* the discouraged team.**

**re•vive** [ri•vīv′] *v.* To bring or come back to life or consciousness: **The doctors can *revive* him once he reaches the hospital.**

**ri•val** [rī′vəl] *n.* A person who tries to equal or outdo another; competitor: **We will be playing our *rival* in the play-offs.**

**rook•ie** [ro͝ok′ē] *n.* A beginner or novice, as in a professional sport: **Although Pamela is just a *rookie*, she scored three times in her first game.**

**ro•ta•ting** [rō′tā•ting] *v.* Turning around, as if on an axis: **The earth is *rotating* constantly.**

**rough•ly** [ruf′lē] *adv.* About; approximately: ***Roughly* 100 students voted in the election today.**

**scaf•fold** [skaf′əld *or* skaf′ōld] *n.* A temporary structure put up to support workers and materials; any raised framework: **The *scaffold* is ten stories high.**

**sculpt** [skulpt] *v.* To form a figure or representation of one from a solid material, as by carving or shaping: **Tomorrow we will *sculpt* a person's head.**

**sed•i•ment** [sed′ə•mənt] *n.* Matter that settles to the bottom of a liquid: **The swift river carried *sediment* into the lake.**

**seis•mo•graph** [sīz′mə•graf′] *n.* An instrument that records the strength and duration of earthquakes: **A *seismograph* in Arizona detected an earthquake in California.**

**sen•a•tor** [sen′ə•tər] *n.* A member of a governing body known as the senate: **The *senator* voted against the bill.**

**se•quel** [sē′kwəl] *n.* A work that continues a story begun in a previous work: **The director's second movie is a *sequel* to his first one.**

**se•quence** [sē′kwəns] *n.* The order of arrangement in which one thing comes after another: **Our teacher asked us to discuss the *sequence* of events in the story.**

**ser•en•di•pi•ty** [ser′ən•dip′ə•tē] *n.* The act of finding good things by accident: **It was *serendipity* that I spotted the ten-dollar bill on the ground.**

**skel•e•ton** [skel′ə•tən] *n.* The internal framework of bones that supports the body of a vertebrate animal: **We studied the**

| | | | | | | |
|---|---|---|---|---|---|---|
| a add | e end | o odd | o͞o pool | oi oil | th this | ə = *a* in *above* |
| ā ace | ē equal | ō open | u up | ou pout | zh vision | *e* in *sicken* |
| â care | i it | ô order | û burn | ng ring | | *i* in *possible* |
| ä palm | ī ice | o͝o took | yo͞o fuse | th thin | | *o* in *melon* |
| | | | | | | *u* in *circus* |

**human *skeleton* in science class.**

**sky•scra•per** [skī′skrā′pər] *n.* A very high building: **The tallest *skyscraper* in Chicago is the Sears Tower.**

**sluice** [slo͞os] *n.* An artificial channel used for transporting water: **The farmer lowered the gate so that no water could pass through the *sluice*.**

**smog** [smog] *n.* A blend of smoke and fog: ***Smog* hangs over the city in the summertime.**

**so•ci•e•ty** [sə•sī′ə•tē] *n.* A group of persons living in a particular place or at a particular time and having many things in common: **Canadian *society* is like that of many European countries.**

**source** [sôrs] *n.* The beginning of a stream or river: **The *source* of the Nile River is Lake Victoria.**

**spe•ci•al•i•za•tion** [spesh′ə•lə•zā′shən] *n.* A topic or subject about which someone knows a lot: **The doctor's *specialization* is heart surgery.**

**spend•ing** [spend′ing] *n.* The act of paying money for goods or services: **If you are going to save money, you need to decrease your *spending*.**

**strive** [strīv] *v.* To make a strong effort: **Please *strive* to learn the vocabulary words.**

**struc•ture** [struk′chər] *n.* A building of any kind: **There is only one *structure* on the farm.**

**sub•ject** [sub′jikt] *n.* The person, thing, or idea that one deals with, as in writing or painting: **The old cabin was the *subject* of the mural.**

**sub•ma•rine** [sub′mə•rēn′] *n.* A ship that operates on or under the surface of the sea: **The *submarine* surfaced less than a mile offshore.**

**sub•se•quent** [sub′sə•kwənt] *adj.* Following in time, place, or order: ***Subsequent* events proved us right.**

**sub•ter•ra•ne•an** [sub′tə•rā′nē•ən] *adj.* Located or happening under the earth: **The *subterranean* tunnels were converted into an extensive subway system.**

**sub•way** [sub′wā′] *n.* An electric railroad that is mainly underground: **We can take the *subway* to the museum.**

**suc•ceed** [sək•sēd′] *v.* To accomplish what is planned or intended: **She will *succeed* in learning all of the multiplication tables before the test.**

**sup•ple•ment** [sup′lə•mənt] *n.* Something that adds to or completes: **The magazine added a *supplement* to cover the recent events.**

**sur•round•ings** [sə•roun′dingz] *n., pl.* The things or conditions around a person or place; environment: **Our school has pleasant *surroundings*.**

**sur•vive** [sər•vīv′] *v.* To remain alive or in existence; outlast: **This kind of tree can *survive* for hundreds of years.**

**tem•per•ate** [tem′pər•it] *adj.* Moderate in temperature: **Many parts of the United States enjoy a *temperate* climate.**

**thrive** [thrīv] *v.* To grow vigorously: **Fish *thrive* in the waters off the coast of Maine.**

**ti•dal** [tīd′(ə)l] *adj.* Of, having to do with, or caused by the tides: **After the tide went out, we splashed in the *tidal* pools.**

**tour•na•ment** [to͝or′nə•mənt *or* tûr′nə•mənt] *n.* A series of matches in a sport or game involving many players or teams: **A chess *tournament* is scheduled for tomorrow after school.**

**train•ee** [trā′nē′] *n.* A person who is being taught how to do something, as in a job: **My sister is a *trainee* at the bank.**

**trans•at•lan•tic** [trans′ət•lan′tik] *adj.* Across or crossing the Atlantic Ocean: **Amelia Earhart was the first woman to make a *transatlantic* flight alone.**

**trans•con•ti•nen•tal** [trans′kän′tə•nen′təl] *adj.* Stretching from one side of continent, or major land mass, to the other: **The first *transcontinental* railroad was completed in the United States in the nineteenth century.**

**trans•late** [trans•lāt′] *v.* To change something written or spoken into another language: **I can *translate* this story into Spanish.**

**trans•lu•cent** [trans•lo͞o′sənt] *adj.* Clear enough to allow light, but not images, to pass through: **The frosted glass in the bathroom window is *translucent*.**

**trans•moun•tain** [trans•moun′tən] *adj.* Crossing or extending through or over a mountain: **Driving through the *transmountain* tunnel was quicker than driving around the mountain.**

**trans•o•ce•an•ic** [trans′ō•shē•an′ik] *adj.* Crossing over or under the ocean: ***Transoceanic* telephone cables lie at the bottom of the Pacific and Atlantic oceans.**

**trans•par•ent** [trans•pâr′ənt] *adj.* Allowing light to pass through so images can be clearly seen; clear: **Windshields are *transparent*.**

**trans•port** [trans•pôrt′] *v.* To carry from one place to another: **The moving trucks will *transport* our furniture to our new house.**

**trib•u•tar•y** [trib′yə•ter′ē] *n.* A stream flowing into a larger stream or body of water: **The *tributary* from the mountain floods the river during springtime.**

**trop•i•cal** [trop′i•kəl] *adj.* Of, having to do with, or located in the hot and humid region known as the tropics: ***Tropical* forests contain many plants and animals.**

**trough** [trôf] *n.* A long, narrow, open container for holding food and water for animals: **The farmer added feed to the *trough*.**

**ur•ban** [ûr′bən] *adj.* Having to do with a city or city life: **We moved away from the *urban* area to live on a small farm.**

**val•ley** [val′ē] *n.* The low area between hills and mountains: **The *valley* was full of shadows in the early morning and late afternoon.**

**va•por** [vā′pər] *n.* Moisture in the form of water droplets floating in the air as mist, fog, or steam: ***Vapor* rose from the lake.**

**veg•e•ta•tion** [vej′ə•tā′shən] *n.* Plant life: **Many large cities have little *vegetation*.**

**ver•te•brate** [vûr′tə•brāt′] *n.* Any animal with a backbone: **Dogs are one kind of *vertebrate*.**

**vi•brant** [vī′brənt] *adj.* Full of energy; vigorous: **Our choir director has a *vibrant* personality.**

**vic•tor** [vik′tər] *n.* The winner, as in a contest or competition: **The judges are about to give a trophy to the *victor*.**

**vig•or** [vig′ər] *n.* Active strength or force;

| | | | | | | |
|---|---|---|---|---|---|---|
| a add | e end | o odd | o͞o pool | oi oil | th̶ this | ə = *a* in *above* |
| ā ace | ē equal | ō open | u up | ou pout | zh vision | *e* in *sicken* |
| â care | i it | ô order | û burn | ng ring | | *i* in *possible* |
| ä palm | ī ice | o͝o took | yo͞o fuse | th thin | | *o* in *melon* |
| | | | | | | *u* in *circus* |

vitality: **For several weeks after his surgery, Trevor couldn't play baseball with much *vigor*.**

**vir•tu•al•ly** [vûr′cho͞o•əl•lē] *adv.* For the most part; practically: **He has read *virtually* every book in the library.**

**vi•tal** [vīt′(ə)l] *adj.* Having great importance; essential: **The oil fields are of *vital* interest to the nation.**

**vi•tal•ity** [vī•tal′ə•tē] *n.* Physical or mental energy; liveliness: **Mr. Reynolds is always energetic and full of *vitality*.**

**vi•ta•min** [vīt′ə•min] *n.* A substance found in food and needed for the body's growth and health: **Many fruits have a lot of *vitamin* C.**

**vi•va•ci•ous** [vi•vā′shəs *or* vī•vā′shəs] *adj.* Full of life and spirit; lively: **My cousins are *vivacious*, always smiling and laughing.**

**viv•id** [viv′id] *adj.* Clear and strong: **Her memories of the awards ceremony were *vivid*.**

**vo•ca•tion** [vō•kā′shən] *n.* A profession, career, or trade: **Is writing his *vocation* or just a hobby?**

**vol•can•ic** [vol•kan′ik] *adj.* Of, produced by, or thrown up from a volcano: ***Volcanic* ash covered the nearby town.**

**vol•un•teer** [vol•ən•tir′] *n.* A person who offers to help or to work without pay: **My father is a *volunteer* for the American Red Cross.**

**wear** [wâr] *v.* To damage or use up: **Too many games of touch football will *wear* the grass in the middle of the yard.**

**weath•er•ing** [weath′ər•ing] *n.* The action of natural elements, such as wind and rain, creating changes, especially in rock or soil: **The *weathering* of the cliffs from the storms concerned scientists.**

**whirl•i•gig** [(h)wûr′lə•gig′] *n.* A merry-go-round: **Many children were lined up to ride the *whirligig*.**

**wind•swept** [wind′swept] *adj.* Swept by or exposed to the wind: **The *windswept* plains looked vast and empty.**

My Own Word List

My Own Word List